THE MEANING AND MYSTERY of BEING HUMAN

Other books by Bruce Larson

The Relational Revolution
The One and Only You
Ask Me to Dance
No Longer Strangers
Thirty Days to a New You
Living on the Growing Edge
Setting Men Free
Dare to Live Now
The Edge of Adventure (with Keith Miller)
Living the Adventure (with Keith Miller)
The Emerging Church (with Ralph Osborne)

THE MEANING AND MYSTERY of BEING HUMAN

Bruce Larson

THE MEANING AND MYSTERY OF BEING HUMAN

ISBN 0-8499-0044-1
Library of Congress catalog card number: 77-83323
Printed in the United States of America

To Sam Elkins
My friend and companion
In many adventures
Who spent the last years of his life
Believing in the dream
Testing the assumptions
And disseminating the conclusions
Of this book

Contents

Acknowledgments

In trying to express my thanks to the many people whose lives and words and works have made this book possible, I feel like the man whose task it was to gather up the feathers from a pillow which had been opened in a high wind. Obviously I am deeply indebted to each person, group, or place mentioned. But I know there are many more from whom I have absorbed much unconsciously, or whose specific contribution has been eliminated in the many revisions this book has experienced in the course of editing my original lengthy research thesis into this present shortened form.

But aside from all these named and unnamed teachers, I would acknowledge my deep debt to another group of people who made this project possible or who contributed to it.

First and foremost is the Lilly Endowment, Inc., whose officers and directors have invested in me and in this project from the beginning. Without their support and encouragement the Group Research and Individual Learning Project dream would still be only a dream. Next I wish to thank Princeton Theological Seminary for the privilege of being a Visiting Fellow on their faculty for these past years and for administering my grant with great care and faithfulness. I am particularly grateful to President James McCord for his personal oversight, correction, and encouragement. Princeton Seminary also graciously consented to host the first week-long Experimental Institute for Human Development, testing with three hundred participants the hypotheses and conclusions of this research project.

I owe much of the success and excitement of the Institute itself to the ten distinguished members of the faculty: Earl Koile, R. D. Laing, Jess Lair, Walther Lechler, Carlyle Marney, James McCord, Keith Miller, Bill and Jean Milliken, and Armand Nicholi.

In the last two years of my project, encouragement and timely support has come from the W. E. Walker Foundation in Jackson, Mississippi.

Finally, I want to acknowledge my co-architects, partners and fellow-seekers during these past years: My wife, Hazel, who has been a collaborator in every phase of the adventure from dreaming to researching, assimilating, writing, editing, and testing; Sam Elkins, retired businessman, full-time partner, adviser, and enabler in all things until his sudden death in January 1977; Keith Miller, my old and dear friend, who has been involved in sorting out the data, building and testing the hypothesis, and in the final preparation of this book; Charles Williams, Vice President at Large of the Lilly Endowment, Inc., and my faithful friend, without whom there would have been no research project; Floyd Thatcher, my more-than-editor, who has given uncounted pre-dawn hours helping to edit the many revisions of this manuscript; Loretta Germann, my incomparable secretary, assistant, and supporter throughout the entire project; David Haney, who acted as a research assistant in Europe and who has helped in many other ways.

Finally I wish to acknowledge those "research assistants," known and unknown, who have launched experiments, both personal and group, based on some of the directions suggested in this book or in the larger thesis on which this book is based. I know some of these experiments were launched as a result of the initial Experimental Institute for Human Development in Princeton. But it is my hope that the thesis now condensed in this present volume will prompt many more such experiments. My own next step is to make this study the basis of building a modular approach system to personal growth, tapping the reservoir of nonprofessionals as lay priests and enablers. May we begin to find, from God's perspective, the mystery and the meaning of being human.

Introduction

In Search of the Grail

Centuries ago, knights of great courage and faith but of questionable judgment set out to look for the Holy Grail. They were convinced that possession of this object would solve most of life's problems—poverty, drought, war, illness, and unhappiness. For generations, whole lifetimes were spent in this search. But they never found it.

Every generation produces its own crop of dedicated knights. They are saddened by the unhappiness and misery that they see about them. They believe that life need not be difficult and unrewarding for so many. Many of these knights believe in a God of love who wills the liberation and fulfillment of all people.

The only thing that changes from age to age is the definition of "the grail." In the Middle Ages men looked for some kind of religious relic left on this earth after the death and resurrection of Jesus Christ. They were sure some tangible object would be found which could be used to liberate and bless people in great numbers. The search for the grail in subsequent centuries has taken many forms. Latter-day knights have set out to bring about advances in the fields of medicine, political reform, and education. In more recent times a great many knights in the garb of psychiatrists, psychologists, and psychotherapists have been trying to find the proper ingredients for a new alchemy of the soul—a philosopher's stone that would turn a lead-colored life into pure gold. While the definition of the grail may vary from age to age, common to all of these knights is a deep conviction that with the right formula life as we know it can be vastly improved for most people in most circumstances.

In recent years I have been under a similar compulsion. I will forever be grateful to the Lilly Endowment, Inc., for undergirding and enabling my own personal search, which up to now has been the great adventure of my life. In the beginning of 1972, I was challenged to do the thing I most wanted to do at that time, and it was simply this: to embark on a study of wholeness—from many and varied points of view. This search might be defined as a search for a correct theological anthropology; that is, a view of man's ideal wholeness from God's perspective. It entailed first examining wholeness from the point of view of a number of existing disciplines in the hope of establishing some sort of clinical syncretism.

Like that of the first knights who searched for the grail, my own motivation is deeply Christian. I believe in a God who loves all men, whose creation reflects that love and who wills an infinitely richer and fuller life for all of us. Since New Testament days, the structure of the Christian church has been largely shaped by its inability to arrive at a conceptual or a theological syncretism—the combination or fusion of different forms of belief. The Eastern Orthodox and Roman Catholic branches of Christendom are the earliest evidence of this. In the sixteenth century, Martin Luther opened the door for the continuing proliferation of denominations. Down through the ages since, the church has sought to heal its divisions by attempting to come to some doctrinal agreement broad enough to reunite all branches of Christendom. But it seems to me it would be more pragmatically possible to come to agreement on the clinical level and move on from there. In medicine, this kind of clinical syncretism is already operating. While there may be radical disagreement on methods of diagnosis and treatment, there is a precise and agreed-upon definition of the well person.

The Christian church may continue to have different emphases and different interpretations of the central truth in Jesus Christ. But I believe it will be a significant day when we have a definition of man's wholeness acceptable to all the branches of Christendom as well as to the doctors, educators, psychiatrists, social workers, and all those in the people serving professions.

I believe God has spread out the pieces of the puzzle of human wholeness and potential throughout many different groups and disciplines, both Christian and secular. The problem is that man has been defined theologically, sociologically, psychologically, psychiatrically, medically, politically, or educationally. The experts in each field seem to have little interest or incentive to think outside their own particular discipline. During the two years of my research I have investigated a number of areas to find these components and to see how they might fit together.

The benefits of such a redefinition of man seem obvious. Today we are rich in equipment, buildings, methodology and resources for the implementing of teaching and training. We are as mobilized for action as a Detroit auto factory. If eventually someone should invent a car which would solve our safety and energy problems, Detroit could turn out a million such models within a year. The production facilities and manufacturing know-how are available. They lack only the prototype. Well, in the same way we are equipped with marvelous institutions for the implementing of ideas that will promote human growth. We seem to be lacking a model. It is to that end that I have undertaken this search.

Let me explain some of my conscious prejudices as I began this quest. I have already mentioned my belief in a God of love who has revealed himself in Jesus Christ. I believe that he is revealing truths and making resources available to help us become more complete and fulfilled persons.

Secondly, I had and have now a growing belief that we are in the beginning of an exciting new age—an age very much like the Renaissance. There is evidence to believe that these times have come upon us with great suddenness. Many of our institutions are crumbling or about to implode. Leaders and creative thinkers in various fields are prophesying this. We are told that just ten years before the Renaissance broke upon the Dark Ages, no one then living guessed that such a time was coming. Like a woman in travail whose baby is delivered without warning in a taxi or a cornfield, the world is pregnant and the labor pains are upon us. It is my hope that this research may somehow hasten the coming of that new age which I believe is already imminent, waiting in the wings to change life for all people upon this globe.

I believe further that this new age will be a time when all the prophecies of the New Testament are fulfilled—a new heaven and a new earth, God with his people wiping away all tears (Rev. 21:1–4). The Old Testament refers to the year of Jubilee; my hope is that the New Testament age coming upon us will be like a permanent year of Jubilee.

Mine is not an isolated hope. Carl Jung stated that in Jesus Christ there is made possible a new rung on the ladder of evolution. Pierre Teilhard de Chardin talks about his dreams for the evolution of a new being and a new society. The New Testament claims that if any man be in Christ he is a new creation. It seems to follow that a new society can come about with the discovery of what it means to be a new creation. My dream is that we are on the verge of such a discovery.

I have one final hope in the area of strategy or methodology. I hope that whatever we learn about human wholeness and how to bring it about will be made available to any lay person without highly specialized training. I have no enthusiasm for a new kind of therapy practiced by a new priestly set, be it psychological, medical, educational, or theological. Because I am a Christian I believe that this strategy is implicit in the New Testament. It describes a fellowship in which every believer is part of a royal priesthood able to minister help and healing to their fellowmen.

I believe basically that we need to see people as resources and not as consumers of resources. Too many educators see people as rows and rows of students for whom they need to provide faculty, schools, and curriculum. Too many doctors see people as patients who need treatment of some kind. Too many preachers see people as parishioners who fill the pews and who need teaching, preaching, or counseling. There will be a resource revolution when all of us view these same people as the very resource for the task to be accomplished.

So much for my prejudices and my hopes at the start of the quest. Certainly it is not a new one. Since the beginning of recorded history, theologians, philosophers, physicians, and novelists have been grappling with the essence of man. Marcel Proust speaks of "that reality far from which we live. . . . The reality that we might die without having known and which is simply our life, real life, life finally discovered and clarified, consequently the only life that has been really lived —that life which in one sense is to be found at any time in all men."

We are all seeking reality. We substitute so many other things for it—things which eventually become an impenetrable barrier to ever finding it. But the great fear in all of us is that we may die before we find what it is to live life as it was really meant to be lived—to discover the meaning and mystery of being human.

Chapter 1

The Pieces of the Puzzle

For more than four years I have been pursuing the elusive concept of wholeness. The first years of the quest took me to a wild assortment of places; from the Big Sur mountains of California to the Black Forest of Germany; from an LSD research center to an educational marathon; from a hospital in the quiet Kent countryside to the Menninger Clinic; from a halfway house in the London slums to a gestalt workshop; from a prestigious university in Amherst to a radical educational center in Cuernavaca; from a psychiatric clinic in Germany to an encounter group in Washington, D.C.; from a transactional analysis institute in California to the renowned Summerhill School in rural England.

I identify with the writer of the Book of Hebrews, who said that time is too short to tell the whole story. My search was a unique one in terms of the people and places examined along the way, but the search itself must be as old as man.

The riddle of what it means to be a person is forever a mystery with which we grapple. Dostoevsky said, "The ant knows the formula of his anthill. The bee knows the formula of his beehive. They do not know their formula in a human way, but in their own way. Only man does not know his formula."

Only Man Does Not Know His Formula

The questions Who is man? and What is the meaning of life? are still unanswered. Yet, while we are a long way from arriving at any acceptable definitions, there is deep within each of us the hint of an idea of what we think it means to be a whole person—happy, functioning, fulfilled. This reality emerges when, as parents, we attempt to give advice to our children based on what we think they *ought to be*. Similarly, the physician treats his patients from an image of what physical wholeness *ought to be*. The psychiatrist treats his client-patient from some form of a working model of wholeness for mind and soul, whether conscious or unconscious. And when friends ask us for advice over a cup of coffee or in a prayer group, we respond to their needs from our own personal experiences and concepts of wholeness.

But even with all of this, the mystery remains. The definition is unclear yet the striving—the search—is ever with us.

As Jürgen Moltmann says, "Man is not a finished creature." His assigned task is to search for his true essence, and that essence is for all of us a "question, a puzzle and a dread." While we may ultimately be able to make our own answer to humanity, that answer is never final, for all existence is an experiment.[1]

Throughout history we see a continuous effort to define

man and what he is meant to be. The purpose of most mythology was to explain man's origins, his essence, and his future. Philosophy and early science, and most particularly religion, it seems to me, attempt to do the very same thing. The Bible helps us to see from God's eyes a revelation of what man is supposed to be. Rabbi Heschel says that many misunderstand the purpose of the Bible. It is not a theology from the point of view of man but rather an anthropology from the point of view of God. Of course he is pointing out, and rightly, that the Bible nowhere proves God. It assumes God is, that he is the Creator of the world and man, and that he is interacting with man.

From Freud to Transactional Analysis

In this twentieth century man has perhaps been even more preoccupied with the riddle of his own nature. Certainly our knowledge of man took a quantum leap when Sigmund Freud discovered the unconscious and mapped it with his classic definitions of the ego, the superego, and the id. Basically, Freud believed that personality is determined in the early years and we simply live out those early conditioning factors the rest of our lives. Behavior can be modified, but we are what our childhood and even prenatal years have made us.

Carl Jung, Freud's contemporary and his student, greatly changed and enlarged this radical understanding of the nature of man. He saw man as a part of a group going back not just generations but centuries. The collective unconscious and the shaping of our lives by the myths and the archetypes play a great part in Jung's attempt to analyze and understand who man is and what he is.

Today, Erik Erikson is the outstanding spokesman for the new school of psychoanalysis which insists man can transcend his childhood, contrary to Freud's beliefs. He talks about the stages of man and believes that man can choose to grow beyond the early pressures and forces that produced him.

In opposition to the Freudians and the Pandora's box of good and evil opened by Freud are the behaviorists—the best-known in our time being B. F. Skinner. Citing Pavlov and others who hold that man is a result of his conditioning, Skinner believes that the individual's pursuit of freedom and dignity is in a large measure the present cause of our social problems. He suggests that we "condition" people out of this concern for their individuality so that the social order might survive.

However, a growing number of our contemporary psychologists and psychiatrists today are embracing a third approach. It is the humanistic approach most frequently associated with Carl Rogers and Abraham Maslow. Maslow, inventor of the term *self-actualization*, speaks about a constantly changing hierarchy of values in our lives. Carl Rogers, believing that all growth and self-actualization must come from within, says we must not tell another what to do or what to be. Our authentic role as friends, therapists, or counselors is to enable and unlock those inner forces which can help each person find his own direction and identity.

While the average layman may have somewhat fuzzy ideas on the differences between a Freudian analyst and a Rogerian counselor, I dare say he knows a good deal more about transactional analysis, the creation of psychiatrist Eric Berne. Thanks to the popularity of *I'm OK—You're OK* by Dr. Thomas A. Harris,[2] a great many Americans are putting transactional analysis theories into everyday use. Actually, transactional analysis represents an unusual wedding of Freudian thought with the theories of Erik Erikson, with the parent, the adult, and the child replacing Freud's id, ego, and superego. Transactional analysis helps a person understand who he is, what his chosen role is, and how the past continues to affect the present. But, the emphasis is that man can change who he is now through self-understanding and by writing new contracts with himself and with the primary others in his life.

The Search Today

So, in the current search for wholeness, we have many approaches to choose from in the various psychiatric or psychological fields from Freud on. In this past decade we have seen the full flowering of the human potential movement. People from all sorts of backgrounds are pursuing wholeness through encounter, yoga, Erhardt Seminar Training, scream therapy, ARICA, to name a few. Even the current emphasis on health foods or natural foods or all-vegetable foods represents an attempt to attain an ideal state through diet.

The findings and conclusions from my own pilgrimage will fill the rest of this book. But throughout the project the most pertinent questions in my mind were, "What is wholeness? What are its components? How would you describe it?" In the next few pages, I would like to share a smorgasbord of answers with you, gleaned from interviews, tapes, or books, quoting a number of people from various disciplines. Some of the answers are surprisingly simple and concise. Bear in mind that those quoted are often equating wholeness with the goal of their particular field, i.e., mental health, physical health, or ideal education, all of which are valid components of wholeness, as far as I'm concerned.

Psychiatry and Mental Health

A study published by the British Medical Association in 1973, *Know Your Own Mind* by H. J. Walton, a professor of psychiatry at the University of Edinburgh, suggests that mental health for the normal person has these ingredients: 1) Self-judgment—a normal person does not belittle himself or overestimate himself. 2) Adjustment—a normal person manages his own affairs. He is neither exploited nor dominated by others. 3) Accurate judgment of reality—a normal person does not wear blinders against awkward facts, does not impute to others motives that they do not have, nor see ghosts, nor imagine slights and insults. 4) Integration—a normal person does not behave in a Jekyll and Hyde fashion.*

However, while one psychiatrist in Edinburgh is urging people to be normal and telling them how, another Scottish psychiatrist is saying, "For heaven's sake, don't be normal. Normal is another name for illness." R. D. Laing, who has worked for many years with schizophrenics, maintains, in the face of much opposition, that possibly schizophrenics are healthier than normal people. He believes that their illness is an attempt to break out of the bonds restricting them and to find some kind of wholeness, a newness of life and role.

A few years ago he and his colleagues did a study on some "normal families" in Glasgow. (The study has not as yet been published.) They chose families in which for at least three years there had been no breakdown of social or economic stability, no death, no birth, no divorce, no bankruptcy, no imprisonment, no major legal entanglements, and no serious physical, emotional, or mental illness. They were all living what they considered a satisfying life. Interviewers were sent to live with these families and tape-record everything that was happening. Before long, the interviewers found themselves suffering from boredom and frustration which resulted in outbursts of intense rage when they returned to their own homes. Laing suggested that these people were reacting to a concertive system of deadness in which everyone seemed to be quite happy and quite dead. All the terminology usually applied to schizophrenia came to mind in describing the subjects of the study: depersonalization, inability to communicate, estrangement, cognitive impairment, and disassociation between thought and effect.

---

* Inversely, Dr. Walton says that some of the features that indicate a person is not functioning normally include: "Inability to work; working so intensively it excludes all other interests; frequent quarrels with workmates or friends; a feeling of being disliked and rejected; overdependence on family for love, approval, and advice; tyrannizing wife and family; morbid jealousy of his or her spouse; neglecting his or her appearance; distaste for sex and lack of tenderness toward a sexual partner."

A succinct definition of wholeness came from the late Eric Berne, the father of transactional analysis and author of *Games People Play*, in a *New York Times* interview: "It is the ability of a person to say 'Yes!' 'No!' and 'Whoopee!' " He went on to explain that people who are sick, or not whole, are people who say, "Yes, but . . . ," "No, but . . . ," and who cannot say "Whoopee!"

The superintendent of a large state mental hospital defined wholeness this way: "Wholeness is simply the ability of the person to cope with his surroundings and relationships." I got this rather classical view of wholeness from Dr. Roy Menninger: "Wholeness is delaying gratification and tolerating pain." And twelve senior clinicians at the Menninger Foundation have isolated five characteristics which to them were most descriptive of whole and healthy people: 1) They had a wide variety of sources of gratification. 2) They could treat others as individuals, not stereotypes. 3) They were flexible under stress. 4) They could recognize and accept their own assets and liabilities. 5) They enjoyed what they were doing—they were active and productive.

Many psychiatrists with whom I have talked seem to agree that there is one universal mark of wholeness in all society: man's willingness to accept danger and risk and even to look for it. Conversely, mental illness is characterized by an inordinate desire to be safe, to be out of danger and to avoid risk.

Wholeness via Gestalt

Fritz Perls, the father of gestalt therapy, had this to say in a lecture at Esalen. "[There are] four important explosions you must be capable of in order to be alive again. The ability to explode in anger, in joy, in grief, and orgasm. This is where the life force wants to work itself out. And, as you probably know, most of our role-playing is designed to use up much of this energy for controlling just those explosions."[3]

The very heart of gestalt, according to Perls, is to find out how you feel now and how you can grow and become what you want to be now. To ask, "Why did this happen?" or "Why am I like this?" or "Why are you like that?" diminishes life. In their positive approach to wholeness, gestalt trainers believe that no one can make another person do or be or feel anything. We have total autonomy and can only *allow* people to hurt us or get to us. Consequently, I am totally responsible for what I feel, for what I do, and what I am. And beginning with that, there is hope that I can take responsibility for my own life and stop blaming others. It is an approach that is making a valid contribution in helping many people to find wholeness.

Wholeness and LSD

Dr. Robert Soskin until recently was the clinical psychologist in charge of administering an experimental LSD program at a psychiatric research center just a few miles from where I used to live. At the center, they are working with alcoholics, terminally ill patients, and professional therapists looking for new insights through the LSD experience. Dr. Soskin gave me his working definition of wholeness. "I think it has a lot to do with a sort of basic faith in the goodness of life. If I can get a person to sort of face into his life and accept whatever that day or the next day brings with a sense of openness, of hopefulness, with a feeling that there is meaning to his experience and to his existence, he is on some kind of path toward growth. Hopefully that might include some concept of the deity of God and that his own life is meaningful."

One of the best definitions of wholeness I've come across came from one of the men who had received LSD treatments. He describes what happened to him in this purely secular situation in this way:

> "I am not the person that I was two years ago. I'm the same person but more and better. I feel a relationship with every-

thing around me. It's not a matter any longer of fitting in, but simply being part of everything. And although I sometimes have fears of getting sick, I know that I could never go back through what seems to be a long journey because there isn't any way to return. Succinctly, I know who I am, I know what I'm doing, I know who is important to me and I like what I am doing. I'm happy and I simply don't think the world is going to hell as so many people seem to. I am once again very aware that there is a supreme power of which all and everything is a part. Most call this power God. I don't think it makes any difference if I call it love. I only wish that the religious forces could obtain those kinds of results." This certainly sounds like the healthiest kind of conversion to me coming out of the drug scene. The statement is by a middle-aged man and is from a case study made by Dr. Soskin.

Medicine and the Whole Person

Dr. Edward Aubert, senior resident physician, described what takes place at Burrswood Hospital in beautiful rural Kent, south of London. "A partnership between medicine and religion is practiced at Burrswood. This partnership is based on the conviction that all genuine modes of healing originate from the divine source of all healing, whether this is mediated by what are called medical or what are called spiritual means. To see divine healing in this wide perspective is a corrective against the danger of seeing it only in the operation of special persons or particular methods. There should be no rivalry between the medical and the spiritual approach to healing—only a sense of partnership."

Burrswood, founded by Dorothy Kerrin, is in my judgment one of the most unique hospitals in England today. It has two resident physicians who are also ordained Anglican priests. The patients receive the finest medical care day by day from these two physicians, from other specialists on call, and from capable nurses and orderlies. But the patients are also prayed for daily by the entire staff. Beyond that, every Sunday those who wish can go to a weekly healing service in which the two doctor-priests perform the laying on of hands and mediate spiritual healing in the name of Christ.

Wholeness-Oriented Education

The urgency of the quest for wholeness is also highlighted by the more outspoken of today's educators. They have some disturbing things to say about education, its past failures and future goals. In a lecture at the University of Massachusetts, Dwight Allen, then Dean of the School of Education, said: "Children of the affluent American society still don't have a very high quality of human life. Our educational aim is to turn that affluence into psychological security for a personal enrichment that gives them a tranquility or a sense that their life is meaningful. Otherwise, we are left with a society which, at its best and at its worst, has in common the quest for a higher quality of life."[4]

And Dr. Arthur Combs and his colleagues at the University of Florida have come up with these goals for a contemporary education: "Education must include more than the acquisition of a few more facts and a faster reading rate. It must be the instrument through which people release the tremendous creative potential that was born into all of us. Whatever methods and materials are needed to do the job, that is education. But this isn't enough. We must also help our young to develop compassion, concern for others, faith in themselves, the ability to think critically, the ability to love, the ability to cooperate with others, the ability to maintain good health, and above all, the ability to remain open to other people and new experiences. This is humanistic education."[5]

A Positive Goal

Viktor Frankl, the Viennese psychiatrist and the originator of logotherapy, got a standing ovation from his San Francisco audience when he proclaimed that while monotheism was a tremendous historical step for mankind, there is a further need for monanthropism, the awareness of the one mankind, of the unity of humanity, and of our own common essence.

I am convinced that society has made some progress since Dostoevsky wrote that "only man does not know his formula." Doctors, psychiatrists, and educators alike are beginning to see that there is more to be done than merely getting the patient functioning or the student making passable grades. Healing and wholeness go far beyond that. Perhaps the goal can best be summed up in this sentence found in the preamble to the World Health Organization's constitution: "Health is a state of complete physical, mental, and social well-being and not merely the absence of disease or infirmity."

Chapter 2

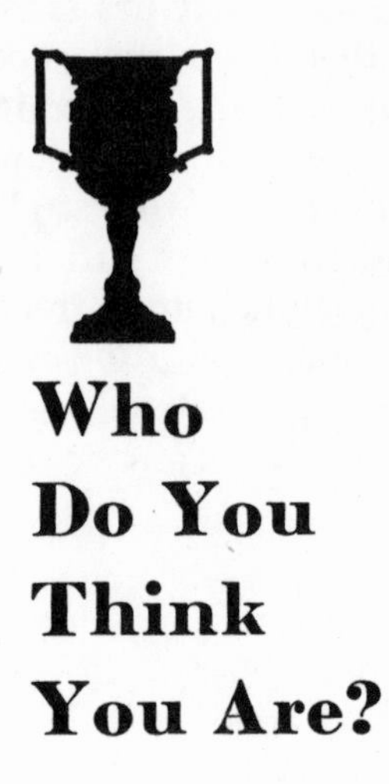

Who Do You Think You Are?

Who am I?

Am I the person I see looking back at me in the mirror? Am I the person that my immediate circle of family, friends and associates tell me I am? Am I what my past has made me? Can I change the child of the past which is still in me? Am I my achievements? Am I my dreams and my hopes? Does my eschatology shape me more than my history? How can I find out what and who I am to be?

Graham Barnes, Director of the Southeast Institute in Chapel Hill, North Carolina, said that problems begin for many of us because of early admonitions from our parents and others to "don't be" and most especially "don't be you." We are all aware of how much religious traditions, schools, and various authority figures can encourage us in our formative years not to be who we are.

The "don't be" admonition is all too recognizable for most of us. We learn early to be mother's little lady or father's little man or a brave participant on the school football team or a member of a church full of nice, polite people, a church which equates faith with niceness or politeness. Using transactional analysis, gestalt, and group therapy, Barnes is helping people to be who they are and affirm who they are and to transcend much of their early negative training.

Psychoanalysis has been one means of seeking to know ourselves and understand our behavior. But Viktor Frankl warned in a recent speech in California that the prolonged use of psychoanalysis or therapy in the unmasking of our motivations must stop somewhere. He further insisted that the man who calls himself an unmasking psychologist must come to recognize that at some point he transcends the unmasking and begins to minimize the man himself. Unmasking after a certain point devaluates and depreciates what is truly human in man.

If the great search is for true identity (who am I?) then a psychological detective who continues to track down the red herrings of defense mechanisms may actually be delaying the discovery of that identity and eventually may even be doing damage to the client he is trying to help. We are not necessarily the people that the past has made us or even the people our psychiatrist tells us we are.

Paul Tournier sounds an even stronger warning about tampering with a person's identity. In an interview with me he said, "I am puzzled by your question of how to help people discover their true identity. It's a utopia to wish to find one's true identity. One never finds it. Tomorrow will probably reveal something in me which will surprise even myself. Identity is not something fixed. Men are in a continuous evolution. The search for identity is like the search for self-actualization. Something utopian. It's our reactions to life which illuminate our identity. But this identity is always being discovered, always being sought. I help people discover a little more about themselves but never a fixed knowledge of themselves as if it were a definite image."

Even though Tournier says we can never ultimately know our true self, his many books point up the fact that the search for self is valid and authentic. If one of the ingredients in wholeness is a sense of personal identity, then we must at least begin that search and pursue it with vigor and integrity.

How Do You See Yourself?

As I see it, the first step in the search for identity is to answer the question, How do you see yourself? The Bible says, "As a man thinketh, so is he." Present-day psychology seems to reinforce that view. You are the number one determining factor in discovering who you are.

"You behave the way you look at yourself," commented Dr. William Glasser, California psychiatrist and author and founder of Reality Therapy, to an audience of educators in Baltimore. This is critical. What you think of the person who looks back at you in the mirror determines largely your behavior in each event of that day. Perhaps you see yourself primarily as a helpless victim. If so, the approach of gestalt therapy is particularly helpful because of its insistence that we must own our own feelings and take responsibility for ourselves. For example, when a group member says, "It hurts," the leader invariably responds, "Don't say *it* hurts. Say *I* hurt." Or, when your responses prompt the leader to suggest that you must be feeling angry, he will not accept an "I don't feel anger" response. Rather you must say, "I will not be angry," or "I choose not to feel angry," or, "I will not allow myself to be angry."

One of the aims of the gestalt approach is for each person to *own* his own feelings and take responsibility for them. We can then say, "This is me." We can then determine within ourselves whether to hurt, to be angry, to love, to care, to leave the job. We are not allowed to cop out with, "*They* did this to me" . . . "*She* makes me angry" . . . "*It* hurts" . . . "*She* makes me unhappy" . . . "*He* causes me pain." According to this approach, each of us is responsible for our own pain, our own misery, our own unhappiness, or our own joy.

Gestalt emphasizes and underscores the conviction that we are not a product of what people have done or are now doing to us. We have the power now to become whatever we want to be; to feel as much love or anger or joy as we want to feel.

One young woman in a gestalt group I was a part of told about a dream she had had persistently since she was a teenager. The setting for the dream was the small town in which she grew up. She dreamed she was a schizophrenic and frequently wandered into the movie theater without paying, using her condition as a cover for being irresponsible. Toward the end of the dream, she was confronted by the theater owner and told that she could no longer come in free. She must pay. As she began to work through this very bizarre dream, it suddenly made sense to her. She saw that she was at the place in her life where she must be willing to pay her way and take responsibility for her actions. There is a price to be paid for the lifestyle she wants.

How Does the World See You?

Another subsequent factor in determining our identity is the image, name, label, or stamp given us by our surroundings and society—in other words, what we believe other people think of us. Most of us participate in many groups simultaneously, each contributing to the jigsaw of our identity. In one sense this data from friends, family, jobs, schools, clubs, churches, and other groups is always changing and often contradictory. But we have come to accept the death of that nineteenth-century mythical man who is alone, needing no one, inner-directed and indifferent to his surroundings. Now we know that people need people and are shaped by people.

Parents influence their children and children influence their parents. But at any given time in one's life there is that special group which has the power, given or assumed, to influence one's self-concept. I can choose those significant persons from among family, friends, or colleagues, but I cannot discount the fact that there will always be such a group and that they are essential to my understanding of my identity.

In Columbia, Maryland, in November 1972, William Glasser spoke to this point. He said that people learn who they are from the people around them. This is why people who fail in school see themselves as failures in all things and, in fact, become so. His own basic philosophy is that public schools provide the data for failure and then grade their own data. He says failure is built in. In his own work in girls' reform schools, he believes that the single most helpful thing to girls who have been released is that they did not fail in his school. For the first time data was coming in to them that they were no longer failures. His own whimsical comment is that you can't fail in reform school because there is no place to send you.

One of the tragedies of old age in our Western society is the accompanying loss of feelings of worth and identity. The senior citizens seem to be receiving feedback to convince them that they are not needed and not wanted. Dr. Victor Sidel, one of the first U.S. physicians allowed to travel in the People's Republic of China, had a good deal to say about the place of the senior citizen in that society. He told me in an interview that there are no retirement or nursing homes for senior citizens. The older members of society still live with their families and are deeply respected. Many of them visit the public schools on a regular basis and teach a course on "How it was in the old days." This is a valid part of his total history for the young Chinese student. According to Dr. Sidel, there is far less senile psychosis among the Chinese simply because the older citizens have self-esteem and a continuing sense of their own identity and worth. Dr. Alex Comfort's lifelong work in gerontology corroborates this. He believes that there is very little genuine physically based senility in senior citizens in America. Most of it is either a self-fulfilling prophecy because of our expectations of what old age will be, or else it is socially induced.

Even the church has been guilty of feeding people negative or indifferent data about their identity. Recently, Dr. Fred Graham published an article in *Christianity Today* suggesting that many churches are doing tremendous harm to their members. A lay person, he says, "looks to his pastor to reassure him of the reality of God and His plan for mankind and gets instead the proclamation of doubt or the glorification of some faddish secular movement, and his spirit, if not the Spirit of God, is quenched."

Dr. Graham proposes three correctives. The first is that "we must not . . . mute the *prophetic* message of judgment of all our social institutions, nor reduce it to a petty moralism." Secondly, the apocalyptic has "an important (if neglected and scorned) part in the biblical proclamation. . . . Finally, . . . we must proclaim that Gospel in whatever ways are available to us and congruent with our responsibilities and personalities under the direction of God's Spirit. . . . Our lives must combine the universality of Paul, the love of John, the immediacy and personal holiness of Matthew and Mark, the open wonder and joy of Luke and Acts." The proclamation of authentically Good News, according to Dr. Graham, ought to be producing discernible positive results in people's lives. We must move from an interpretation of the gospel that says, "Worm that I am" to one that says, "You are made in the image of God."[1]

You Are What You Do!

A third factor in our search for identity is our behavior—what we are doing. Far more important than how we see ourselves or how society sees us, this third area is where we have the greatest control over our own identity. *We* can decide what *we* will do, within very large limits, and by the very act of doing we become something. A colleague of mine, David Haney, gives us some insight on this point. "What made Moses Moses? The fact that he found the will of God and did it. If Moses had stayed in Pharaoh's court, if Moses had stayed in the deserts of Midian, or if Moses had refused to go to Pharaoh, then he would not have been Moses. What we are is related to what we choose to do. We are given gifts, and in our acceptance of those gifts, we become. God created us and he created us with a purpose. As we discover the purposes of God, and begin to fulfill them, that is the process of self-actualization."

All of us understand what Haney is saying about the relationship of job, involvement, responsibility, and mission to identity. Several years ago I made a job change. From being the head of an organization with staff oversight, fund-raising responsibilities, and a load of administrative duties, I began the research project on which this book is based. My "staff" shrank to one half-time secretary. Research replaced administration. Listening and asking questions replaced lecturing and teaching. Immediately my chronic backache stopped without my having to purchase a new mattress. I have not had a cold in four years. Praying became a joy rather than an awesome responsibility. My change of jobs made me glad of who I was. It felt good to be me.

Body Language

Your own body is also a factor in the search for identity It tells you who you are, and who you are is reflected by your body. The phrase *body language* indicates that we can read a great deal about a person's ego, identity, and self-concept from the way he stands, sits, walks, or looks. Your body and you are inseparable, and it is imperative to understand what the body is trying to say to us.

At a seminar at the University of Maryland in November 1973, William Shutz said, "I can't really be an integrated, whole person unless I am really in touch with my whole body, unless I accept it all, unless I like it all and am aware of it. Everybody has areas of his body that even he isn't aware of and doesn't understand. If there are parts of your body where there is no sensation or no understanding or no acceptance you are incomplete. That part doesn't belong to you. It just isn't yours. So the more you become integrated, the more you become in touch with yourself and the more you have of yourself to give to others."

The Place You Live

Our immediate geography is also a means of providing insight into our search for identity. The place we live has something to say about who we are. For the most part, even the person who feels trapped in his surroundings by his income or job or family responsibilities really has choices. Within certain limits of income there are an infinite number of kinds of places where we can live and, in extreme cases, where we can change jobs in order to live in a more satisfying environment. Most of us have a great deal of choice in terms of deciding where we will live.

Conversely, however, the place we have chosen often imposes on us a certain identity, perhaps one we are striving for. Answering questions about where I live and why I live there, why it is meaningful, and where I would live if I could choose to move can produce useful clues about who I am.

A story I heard R. D. Laing tell is helpful on this point. A family of shopkeepers moved from Liverpool to London some eighteen years ago. The suburb in North London in which they settled was about an hour and a quarter from the West End of central London. Laing asked the father of this family why he had moved to London, thinking it must have been for economic reasons since it was after the war and things were tight in Liverpool. Without a moment's hesitation, the father replied, "In order to be near the center of things." Asked exactly what he meant by the center of things, he said, "The changing of the guard at Buckingham

Palace." "How often have you been to see the changing of the guard at Buckingham Palace?" Laing asked. Actually, in eighteen years the man had never been to see the changing of the guard, but he liked to know he could go if he wanted to.

There are many ways to interpret our choice of a place to live. All of us are aware of family or friends who have built homes close to the old family homestead where mother and father still live, even refusing job promotions that would take them away. Conversely, others have moved as far from home as geographically and financially possible. Some choose to live all of their lives in the modest "first home," even though they have become wealthy and could live "on the hill." Others always live beyond their means, carrying mortgages they can't afford. Some will sacrifice precious hours of commuting to live in the country; art lovers may choose to live austerely, investing instead in precious works of art; sometimes city dwellers who could afford a penthouse prefer the bleakness of a flat in the inner city. Unless we are severely restricted economically, the choice of a place to live is seldom accidental, even though it is often meaningful to pretend to ourselves that we are trapped by circumstances.

How Do You See Others?

A final and intensely important clue to our own identity is found in how we see other people. How we see others, how we interpret their motives, and how we relate to them gives us a picture in living color of who *we* are.

A number of experiences in National Training Labs were helpful to me in this area. One of the techniques they used to help those in the group who were having tense relationships is to encourage face-to-face, or back-to-back, dialogue. I can remember being back to back with someone called Ron who bugged me considerably. We were talking about why we bothered each other. A number of times the trainer said, as he did all through the workshop, "Bruce, what does the Ron in you say to the Bruce in you right now?" And, "Ron, what does the Bruce in you say to the Ron in you?" This was most meaningful to me because I found that what I did not like about Ron and what made me fearful of him was actually a part of me projected onto him. Ron handled his insecurity by being overly friendly, trying to win quick friendships. He was loud and boisterous and quick with humor and sarcasm. He seemed to need to prove that he knew more than he did on many subjects. In other words, the external Ron was enough like me to arouse the internal Ron inside me.

In any true search for identity, I have to think through how I feel about the mother in me, the father in me, the brother in me, the friend in me, the enemy in me. All the significant others in my life exist not only externally, but internally. The way I relate to the parts of me they represent will affect how I relate to them.

Life Is a Journey

It seems to me that in the search for identity, each person is on a journey. The journey has a past—our history. It has a present—the current role we have chosen to enact. And it has a future—a destiny toward which we are headed.

First, our history. Where did I come from?

It has been said that if you haven't come to terms with your history you are condemned to repeat it. I am sure that many of us choose not to remember our history because it is painful and threatening. But if we choose not to understand our psychological, spiritual, emotional, and dynamic history, in a sense we will repeat that history over and over again in the present and in the future.

Fritz Perls, in *Gestalt Therapy Verbatim,* says that the great error of psychoanalysis is in assuming that the memory is reality and that these memories are identical with our history. Actually a memory is an abstraction. We take these abstractions and file them away and call them memories. If these memories are unpleasant to our self-esteem, we change them. He quotes Nietzsche, who said, "Memory and pride were fighting. Memory said it was like this and pride said it couldn't have been like this. And memory gives in." So many of our memories are exaggerations and projections and a means by which we deceive ourselves.[2]

In the past two years I have asked any number of psychiatrists, clinical psychologists, and therapists which was most essential to finding true identity—understanding the past, the present, or the future. Without exception, I was told, understanding the present is by far the most important. Dr. George Phillips, Superintendent of Crownsville State Hospital in Maryland, said that to get well the patient must be helped to handle the present, to improve his relational ability in the now. Secondly, he needs to understand his destiny and his dream for the future. Coming to grips with his personal history is the least important aspect, according to Dr. Phillips.

The director of a large psychiatric research center gave me this wise answer when I asked about the relative importance of the past, present, or future in dealing with a troubled person. "It depends on the patient," he said. "For example, if a patient comes in who is dangerously ill and about to do violence to someone, you wouldn't ask him how he feels about his father." He mentioned that for some people the past is totally forgotten and they can't even remember very much of their early life. Other people can remember every detail of their growing up, and constantly itemize and rehearse it. Neither condition is in itself a sign of health or illness.

One of the most effective tools we have today for understanding the role of the past in our present is transactional analysis. Here the present is emphasized, and we are made aware of the choices we have right now. But we are also helped to sort out who we are and where we have come from. According to transactional analysis, the past lives in us through parent, adult, and child tapes we have stored up and with which we are dialoguing in all of our present situations. So transactional analysis is a tremendous tool for helping a person to understand himself and to see that he is acting the role of the parent, child, or adult in each encounter. This gives him a basis for making some choices about what to do with the past.

Let's think now about the present in terms of role—the part that I am playing right now. At this point I am not referring to role in terms of a job or as father, mother, student, or committee member. Rather, I am speaking of a role in terms of my image, the kind of person I project—the go-getter, the party boy, the strong silent type, the sexpot, the martyr. There are an infinite number of life patterns and personality variations a person can project.

Which role are you in? You can probably get a clue by pinpointing what it is you want people to think about you. For example, what epitaph would you like on your tombstone, or what do you hope will be said about you after your death? This is probably the role you are projecting. Once we can honestly say, "This is what I want people to think of me," then we can begin to deal with the dynamics that have made us choose this role. Once I'm aware that I am playing a role, I can choose to continue in it, modify it, or change it.

But, contradictory as it may sound, it is also true that to some degree roles are often thrust upon us. I'm not always free simply to choose. I react to the pressures and expectations around me.

The third dimension of our present journey, or search for identity, requires claiming our destiny or trying to discover our future. Certainly my identity is shaped by the willful direction my life has taken. My conscious goals and my unconscious goals are a tremendous force in determining my present identity.

One clinical psychologist at the Menninger Foundation felt that the greatest gift he could give someone in trouble was the belief that they had a destiny and a future and a contribution to make. He said, "I have great faith in people's possibilities and potentials. I think the communication of that faith in people's strength can give them a lot of strength. If we view people as a mass of weakness and pathology, that doesn't give them a hell of a lot of strength to go on. I try to communicate to another person, 'Look, you really have it in you to make it big. You really do.' I think that is the greatest gift you can give somebody."

The futurologists have opened new horizons for all of us by telling us that we are no longer trapped by linear thinking, which says that you can project the future from the past. Instead, they say, the future is systemic. We have a number of choices about what we can become. The determining factor is not the past but our hope for the future. Our expectations about the future as a nation or world or as a person are powerful shaping forces. My sense of destiny will determine more who I am and what I become than does my past history or my present entanglements. People are unpredictable. A genuine sense of destiny frees us to become all we are meant to be.

Even theologians are speaking of the world as a land of unlimited possibilities. A "theology of hope," for example, conveys the idea that our future is self-determined. If the world in which we live were a closed system, there would be no place for a theology of hope. If nothing new can happen, there is no real future. Without hope, man is in a self-prison, a tiny wheel in the world machinery. A society in which man has no chance to define his own future is a closed and repressive society.

While futurologists and theologians acknowledge the place of hope on the world scene, a sense of hope about the future is just as crucial to every individual. Without a chance to shape our future and to believe in it, we die in the present. The New Testament message is that, in giving us his love, God gives us a sense of his future and our future together. Our freedom to live in the now depends on our sense of hope in an ever-expanding future.

Celebration Is the Barometer

We are all on a journey from the past into the future, with our emphasis on life in the present. If the purpose of that journey is to find our true and authentic identity, what barometer can we use to indicate that we have at least begun to uncover the true self? As friends, parents, doctors, or therapists, how can we recognize that the person in this search is beginning to make contact? My response to that question is, "If you are finding your real identity, there is joy, celebration, and self-affirmation."

In a book entitled *Man's Concern with Holiness,* Philip Caraman, a Jesuit, writes this in a chapter entitled "Holiness in the Catholic Tradition": "Happiness is a characteristic of all saints both in life and in death. 'The sad saint,' said Francis de Sales in a much-quoted phrase, 'is a sad sort of saint.' The priest or nun who has an authentic calling is not lastingly affected by gloom or depression. Even the sense of humor the saints possess is enhanced by grace. Many such as Philip Neri were incurable jokers and kept their childlike charm unspoiled. Francis of Assisi manifestly took great pleasure from God's animal creations. He was conscious all the time of the concern of God for all that came from his hands. The joy he always manifested makes him attractive to Christian and pagan alike."[3] Whether in a gestalt workshop with Fritz Perls or in a spiritual quest for true holiness, we must come to grips with our true identity. And whether we believe we find it within, or that it is the gift of God, I believe that true identity must be accompanied by hilarity and joy.

Admittedly, it isn't easy to celebrate—to be happy and optimistic. The poet Mark Van Doren wrote, "It takes courage to be happy." We must find the courage somewhere, whatever the source, to believe that, given our unique past, our present role, and our chosen destiny, we can be happy and we can share that happiness. The unfolding discovery of the authentic person in each of us is in itself a cause for celebration.

Chapter 3

What Do You Really Want?

The principal question in life, according to one psychiatrist whom I interviewed, is not Who am I? since I change from time to time, but rather, Where am I going? My future and my goals determine who I am more than anything else.

But how can I find what my goals are, let alone what goals I am recommending or encouraging for others? It seems to me that the pursuit of wholeness must include an attempt to understand my own values and priorities. And these are seldom clear-cut and obvious.

Even the goal of self-actualization expounded by Abraham Maslow comes by an indirect route, according to Dr. Viktor Frankl in this comment: "There is no objection against self-actualization, but self-actualization in the final analysis is only available and can only be obtained to the extent that a man has embarked in the first place on fulfillment of higher meaning and purpose. Thereby one is actualizing himself without caring for it. On the other hand, to the extent to which one directly is heading for self-actualization one loses ground. Self-actualization is achieved by not aiming at it. It is a by-product."[1]

Then he goes on. "Now Maslow who so beautifully has described self-actualizing personality types in the last years has come to recognize this fact by pointing out that self-actualization can best be obtained by devotion and dedication to a selfless goal . . . rather than directly caring for an attempting of this phenomenon."

In a lecture, Maslow himself said that every single self-actualized person he had ever met or read about or heard of had a cause, a vocation—a calling.

In an interview, Paul Tournier had this to say about self-actualization: "It seems that self-actualization never comes all by itself. It is the consequence of other things. If one's goal is to achieve self-actualization, then there is the risk of not finding it because one takes, therefore, a rather selfish attitude. And it's only in forgetting one's self that one can find true self-actualization. Self-actualization is a consequence rather than a goal. It is not something that one realizes. Anyway, it is not at all my aim to achieve self-actualization, but I seek to help each man achieve a natural harmony where each one can be self-actualized in his own way, without trying to make this a goal or an enterprise."

Tournier speaks of self-actualization as the result of self-denial and self-forgetfulness, while Maslow and Frankl consider it by the by-product of a great consuming vocation or goal. But all three are in basic agreement.

Goals and Values for the Christian

For those of us who are Christian, there seem to be some rather clear-cut goals and values. Surely we would all agree that to keep the Ten Commandments and practice the Beatitudes is the explicit and implicit task of the Christian. However, a friend of mine has just concluded an interesting study on the subject of cheating. He claims he has conclusive evidence that Christians cheat more than non-Christians in the classroom. By "Christians" he means authentic church members, people who consciously affirm that they belong to a Christian church and are identified with it and are the products of its teaching. I don't know how he will explain this phenomenon, but I would guess that while personal honesty is a basic teaching of the Christian church, there is a more insistent message being communicated subliminally. That message is, "Son (or daughter), you must succeed! You'd better make it in the real world. By making it, you are certain to win the approval of your parents, the church, and society. Further, your success will be proof that God loves you!"

It seems we are forced to face the reality that in groups as small and flexible as the family or as large and tradition-bound as the U.S. Military Academy, the professed and outward values are often in conflict with the deeper, unspoken ones. The same syndrome is evident in the church in that grace and forgiveness are proclaimed, but there are still many Christians who interpret being right with God in terms of the "victorious life," which assumes that sufficient power and guidance from God will insure against human failure. If the "victorious life" is the end product, then it is understandable that any means of getting there (e.g., cheating) is preferable to failure.

Many years ago an old friend of mine turned his ancestral home in London into a place where Christians could live and work together—a sort of commune before there were communes. He wanted this to be a place where both burdens and costs would be shared equally. At least 25 percent of the guests would be people with deep emotional or psychological problems, and they would be ministered to by the other members of the community.

I visited Ron recently and asked him to evaluate the experiment after all these years. His first comment was a shocker. He said he has come to question the integrity of a good many theologically conservative Christians. With literally dozens, possibly hundreds, of people coming through his home over the years, he had concluded that often the more orthodox and pious members of the community were the least willing to carry burdens of others and to live up to their commitments financially, socially, or morally. He says, "The people who have spoken most of Jesus have been those who have received the most from this house and the people in it and who have put the least in."

Now, I believe in the need for Christians to bear witness verbally to their faith. Good deeds and a loving, kind disposition cannot of themselves be a proclamation of the Good News—the incarnation, death, and resurrection of the God-man. But at the other end of the spectrum, we are all aware that excessive verbalization can become a substitute for authenticity. I love the whimsical comment Jimmy Carter's mother, Miss Lillian, made regarding Jimmy's public pledge that he would never lie to us as President. "It troubles me!" she confided. "If a person never lies, he never has to say he will never lie. Everyone knows it!" Miss Lillian was suggesting that our words cannot replace our deeds. As enthusiastic witnesses for what and whom we believe, we must be on guard that our integrity, generosity, and sense of responsibility match our words. Our true values and goals are exceedingly easy for others to read.

Defining an Adequate Goal

We're only just beginning to realize how the understanding of our goals and priorities affects our everyday lives. The Bible tells us we cannot serve God and mammon. Viktor Frankl takes this even farther and suggests that people become what they worship. I heard him say, "If you worship the computer, you become an unfeeling computer. If you worship the military, you become military. If you worship the industrial, you become a producer and consumer." He believes our goals and the things we want and aspire to have magnetic power over us.

A few years ago an extremely fascinating study was done of a select group of one hundred Harvard graduates who had achieved a "successful" life by all accepted normal standards. It was discovered that a huge percentage were complaining of a deep sense of futility and despair because of the apparent meaninglessness of their lives. What they apparently thought they wanted and had striven for did not bring them satisfaction or wholeness.

What an astounding conclusion! But it certainly illuminates a basic test to determine the adequacy of our primary goal in life: Does it bring fulfillment when it is achieved?

This is a time when educators particularly are sorting out their goals and values, mindful of past failures and present inadequacies. At a 1974 seminar at the University of Florida on creative teaching, one leader said that there are two things that make you a good teacher. You must like yourself and you must like the people you teach.

Now how do you measure how much you like other people? Certainly not by how nice you are to them. And how do you measure how much you like yourself? Certainly not by self-indulgence. But as difficult as these qualities are to measure, the statement was enthusiastically endorsed by all the teachers at the seminar, even though they did not know how to evoke these qualities or to encourage them in a potential teacher.

In the many hours, days, and weeks that teachers spend with children in our schools, all kinds of values are being learned and absorbed by students. Educator Dwight Allen said at a conference at the University of Massachusetts in 1973, "You know, when that little kid is in the algebra class, one of the things he is learning, hopefully, is algebra. But he is also learning about himself and his self-image, and he is learning how to deal with other people. He is learning how to deal with me (as a teacher) and to respond to what I want him to respond to or to figure out how to get around what I want him to respond to. He is learning how to establish social relationships, how to accept responsibility, how to dodge responsibility. He is learning a whole lot of things of which algebra is only one. And the school pretends that it is only teaching algebra!" The schools are a tremendous force in shaping all of us and in shaping our children and our children's children. Values are inculcated, disseminated, and passed on, and this is quite incidental to the curriculum.

I have little doubt that most of us are looking for something to give ourselves to: a purpose, a vocation, a calling, a goal. The great task of the Christian church is to call people to an authentic purpose emanating from a response to God. This authentic purpose is mostly tied to finding our true self and vocation. Too often, though, we have proclaimed a problem-solving gospel. Acting from the base of a moral theology, we have taught that an adequate faith will help Christians to solve difficult problems. I am convinced, though, that to be a whole human being full of authentic faith does not diminish or remove problems.

Conscious and Unconscious Goals

I have been impressed on a number of occasions by the apparent direct correlation between the appropriation of authentic goals and the recovery of health. It is as though the absence of purpose leads to irresponsible behavior which in turn makes the body break down or rebel. In a week-long gestalt workshop my wife and I attended, a young woman came to believe in God—a moral God who presses for sexual purity. This woman, sexually permissive by both the group's observation and her own confession, chose to change her lifestyle and was immediately "healed" of a chronic spastic colon. I will never forget her words on the last day of our session at Esalen: "No wonder I've had this illness in my body. I have been denying God's will for me. I have not known there was a God. I've found him and I intend now to live by a new set of values."

Now, I don't know if her sudden cure lasted after she left Esalen and went back to her daily life. I would like to believe that it did. I know only that someone was able to talk to her about ultimate values without moralizing, and this brought a remarkable physical change.

Yet there is a deep resistance in many quarters to any kind of goal-setting, particularly for other people. A few years ago I had an opportunity to visit Summerhill, the creative school in England. Summerhill somehow embodies a denouncement of some of society's most accepted values. Their fervor for eliminating any kind of competition and promoting cooperation is perhaps the most outstanding conscious value at Summerhill. In a visit to some classes, I observed a horsemanship class being taught to young pre-teenage girls. I must say, there seemed to be all the usual pressure on certain students to do as well as the rest of the class. So, even though Summerhill's conscious aim is to avoid competition, the actual teaching of at least that class was based on a subtle, competitive approach that exhorts students to keep up with the class or even surpass it.

It is important for those of us in quest of wholeness and personal authenticity to understand as best we can the values and goals operating in our lives. While one does not always act on those values, they are still dynamic.

A Simple Rule of Thumb

Again, Dwight Allen gave some helpful clues in the pursuit of this idea. He said at that same conference mentioned earlier that each of us has certain judicial limits for his life. There are first of all those things we will tolerate. Beyond the things that we will tolerate there are the things that we will be enthusiastic about and want to promote. And at the extreme other end are those things that we simply will not tolerate.

This gives a very simple rule of thumb to understand the values that work in each person's life. 1) What are the things that you absolutely will not tolerate and that you will risk a great deal to put a stop to? 2) What kinds of behavior can you tolerate even though you don't approve? 3) What are those values that you yourself will trade your money, your time, your reputation, your health, and your very life to propagate?

Finding Your Level of Need

Another creative way of helping people to understand themselves in the area of values and goals comes from the work of Abraham Maslow and his outline of a hierarchy of needs. Maslow says that a person's most basic need is physiological —the need for survival, to simply exist and stay alive in the world. The goals of those in danger from physical disease, hunger, cold, or lack of housing are simple. They include feeding the body, keeping it alive, warm, and clothed. When these needs have been taken care of and are no longer a problem, Maslow says, a person automatically has new needs, and these are for safety—to guard against loss of money or health and to protect one's self from thieves and other dangers. Money in the bank, a lock on the front door and taking vitamin pills are all part of meeting one's needs at the safety level.

If these needs are met, the next level of need includes love and affection, or what we might call intimacy or belonging. You need to have people find you worthwhile, attractive, enjoyable, and worthy of love. Next we can move up the ladder of Maslow's hierarchy to the need for esteem. We need to feel important in the eyes of our peers. We need to wear clothes that say we are "sharp," well-dressed, attractive, and affluent. Our house, our office, the car we drive, the honors and degrees we receive—all of these things feed this higher level of need.

Now Maslow says that, after these esteem needs are met,

we move into the need for self-actualization. This is the desire to become everything that we are meant to be. But this level can only become a conscious goal when the four earlier needs have been met. Obviously, we all can move from one level to the other at any time depending on circumstances. Someone moving into the self-actualization area of life may change his values radically if a doctor's examination reveals a terminal illness. At that point he may be willing to trade safety, belonging, esteem, and self-actualization simply to exist and stay alive.

In his later years, Maslow went on to talk about two more levels of need beyond self-actualization. A sixth need is to know and understand. This is the need of the potential philosopher in all of us to see life and to understand it, to find God and first causes. And even beyond that is the creative, aesthetic need for music, art, literature, or whatever happens to speak to each individual's aesthetic need. But again, even the person at the top of Maslow's hierarchy who is busy surrounding himself with beauty and creativity suddenly finds a whole new set of values when he discovers his wife is having an affair or his child has been arrested.

Inherited Values

To understand values and how they operate in our lives it is helpful to know where they originated. This is essential in separating our own true values from the values of the groups to which we belong. It's almost impossible to grow up as a member of a family without adopting the family's values as our own, consciously or unconsciously. Much of adolescent rebellion is an attempt to affirm our own values as over against those of the family. In spite of this time of rebellion, those early values tend to remain and become a part of our adult identity. Schools, churches, and society in general are all shaping forces for our values and goals. In all of the groups to which we belong, however static or dynamic, we are exposed to values and we assume certain values simply by belonging. Our own search for wholeness can be greatly hampered unless we can separate those that are collected from various groups and those that are authentically our own.

In the Western world, society has said certain things about life and how it should be lived, and we are all subject to these values, constantly absorbing them and being shaped by them. Our values come then from what society says is important and what society says is "right." Our institutions and our laws underscore what the majority really believes, and this is, of course, transmitted to all of us.

Without question, the schools are the most powerful tools society has in the shaping and inculcating of values. If we think of the school as a place where objective content is taught and there is no transmitting of values, we are naïve. Every teacher transmits personal values to the students. Teachers and students spend many hours together in the classroom every day. And while such subjects as religion, ethics, and life goals may never be discussed, the students have ample opportunity to sense what their teacher really believes through attitudes and behavior. If the teacher has an authentic relational ability, the transference of ideas and values is eminently successful. It is impossible for students—children or adults—not to be challenged and changed by the values of a respected, dynamic teacher.

According to John Holt, one of our creative and revolutionary educators, today's schools fill three major functions in our society. First of all, the school has a custodial function. Society cannot allow its young to run loose on the streets while the majority of its citizens are working at adult jobs, so they are taken off the streets and put into places of confinement to keep them from breaking things, running rampant, or hurting themselves or others. The second function of the school is to rank or grade or label students. Society needs to put labels on its citizens to indicate who is of worth and who is not, who excels and who does not. As students go through our Western schools they come out with an ingrained sense of where they belong. Are they average, are they excellent, are they failures? The school takes care of this kind of classification. The third and much more subtle function has to do with indoctrination, with getting people to accept the system. Holt talked with the head of a firm which hires only college graduates. He asked, "Is there anything a person learns in college that makes him better qualified to do the work required here?" "No" was the answer. "But we do believe that anybody who can submit to the boredom and routine of four years of college life will not be a trouble-maker in our company."[2]

That certainly is a damning indictment, and whether it is true or not, the fact remains that most of us in the course of our school years have absorbed a great many hidden but dynamic values that society has imposed on us through these very institutions. Our job is to sort out these assumed and absorbed values from those that come from within our inner being and that we can affirm as truly our own. I cannot be a whole person if I live by the values imposed by other people or by my culture unless I can honestly embrace those values as my own.

Your Personal Values

As I discover and sort out those values that are truly my own, I can do one of two things: I can affirm them even though they may run counter to the values endorsed by the institutions to which I belong, including my family, my church, my school; or, aware of what my real values are, I can choose to change them if they are no longer meaningful.

The Pankey Institute for Advanced Dental Education in Miami, Florida, is a most unusual post-graduate dental school.[3] The professors there base their approach on the premise that dentists have at least four needs. 1) The dentist needs to rekindle his dwindling enthusiasm for his career. 2) He must acquire a more positive self-image. 3) He must readjust his priorities in his life. 4) He needs to find a pathway to greater personal, professional, and financial success.

One dentist has said, "Let's face it. The practice of dentistry can be tedious, boring, frustrating—sometimes a killing experience. Or it can be one of service, joy, excitement, fulfillment and self-realization. No words can express what Dr. Pankey's new approach meant to me." In the words of one of their staff, the school's basic goal is "to change dentists from tooth dentists to people dentists." In other words, patients are not just a mouthful of teeth.

I think there is a powerful lesson to be learned from this radical approach in dentistry which could well apply to most businesses and professions. When people decide to learn how to love themselves and their work and the people they work with, they are espousing powerful and life-changing values.

Paradoxically, though, in spite of all we have discussed about the importance of transmitting values, no one can really give another person a meaning for his life. Dr. Viktor Frankl and his colleagues affirm this fact. Dr. Frankl said in the lecture referred to earlier in this chapter, "The unique meanings inherent in all those unique life situations that together form one string must be found. They cannot be given. No psychiatrist, no educator, no professor, no teacher can instill meaning—can prescribe meaning. The only thing he may give is his personal, his existential example of his own dedication and devotion to the great cause of truth finding or to scientific research."

So in helping others to find meaning, we can only provide a model, and a model does not moralize or teach or instill values. But as teachers, parents, or preachers, we can model a reality of life which may deeply affect another person.

The Importance of Dialogue

Dialogue can be enormously helpful in discovering and understanding our values and goals. It is difficult to arrive at what our true values are by reading and introspection. In dialogue with another person who is listening, caring, asking questions, and in some way holding us accountable, we can begin to understand who we are and what we believe. For a long time psychologists have been saying, "Behavior that is observed changes." Perhaps this is why dialogue with someone else on a regular basis is so helpful. For example, if I know that the person with whom I am in dialogue is going to ask me pertinent questions about what I am doing, my behavior will change simply because I am now reporting it to someone who can view my actions with objectivity. And the objectivity of another person is so important because frequently my own motives are beyond my understanding. There are so many quirks in my personality that are not readily apparent to me.

The accountability that comes from dialogue helps provide motivation for change. A classic experiment was conducted by McClelland and Atkinson in the area of motivation. They selected a number of five-year-old children, gave them some ring quoits, and told them to throw them on the peg. But they didn't tell the children how far away to stand. Now there was something in each child that predisposed him to either failure or success. The one who moved right up and stood above the peg couldn't miss as he dropped one ring after another right on the peg. Actually, though, his phony success produced personal failure. On the other hand, children who stood so far away that it was impossible to ring the peg also insured their own failure. Only those children who could handle success were able to stand at a reasonable distance and throw the quoits even though they often failed.

The dynamics behind my predisposition for failure, for example, may be forever hidden to me without some kind of objective dialogue. Dialogue at its best involves helping another interpret his life without imposing goals or values. Again, I am indebted to Viktor Frankl for a story about the crucial role that skillful dialogue played in one man's search for meaning. In a San Francisco lecture, he told about an old general practitioner who came to him because he could not reconcile himself to the death of his wife. Frankl asked the doctor, "What would have happened if not your wife but you had died first?" The old doctor said, "Oh, how terrible this would have been for her. How much she would have suffered." Then Frankl was able to point out, "You see, doctor, your wife has been spared the suffering, but it's you who are sparing her the suffering as it were and you have to pay for this by surviving and mourning her." At that moment the man's attitude changed. His suffering took on meaning, he was released from his depression, and he began to live again. The simple, obvious words of a friend gave him a whole new interpretation of the meaning of his own suffering.

What Do You Really Want?

Finally our behavior patterns can give us a clue to our unconscious values. Suppose I am usually tardy or absent from a group which meets weekly for prayer and Bible study. Loving acceptance of my behavior by the group may be of little help to me. But open confrontation by the group may help me grapple with whether or not I really believe in prayer and Bible study. Perhaps I would prefer to use the time for something else.

Now, how are we to select those persons or groups with whom to associate that will help us discover our own values and goals? Success is the progressive realization of a goal, but the corporate goal is never identical with the goal of each of the members of the group. To find the right group I've got to find a group that does not deflect me from my own true goals as I understand them. Rather, it should enhance them. Each person has a different goal, and a successful group is one that will help each person find his own goal in the context of the group's goals and not subordinate that goal for the good of the group. This to me is one of the measures of authentic Chrstian fellowship. It is not a fellowship that insists I sublimate my individual goals for the group goal, but rather one that says, "Along with pushing our corporate goal, we will try to help you finally become the unique person that your goals and values dictate."

Understanding what I believe and what I want in life is no easy thing. But if I am on the road to wholeness and pursue it for myself or for others there is no way I can avoid coming to grips with the business of understanding authentic values and priorities and goals.

Chapter 4

Learn to Throw Your Weight Around

It seems to me that a primary step to wholeness is to recognize and understand the power game—what I am doing to people; what I allow them to do to me. Dr. Thomas Szasz, controversial psychiatrist and teacher at the State University of New York, puts it this way, "Wholeness, self-realization, has a great deal to do with the exercise of one's powers in some way which is spiritually satisfying to the person himself."

In a sense all of life is a power struggle. And sex, talent, wealth, fame, position, beauty are some of the factors in the equation that ultimately add up to "power." In the family setting, the struggle emerges when the child is still very young. Frequently, admonitions to "eat," "go potty," or "stop that" are met with clenched fists and howls of anger.

In marriage the struggle for power is an underlying source of conflict. Paul Tournier, in his book *The Strong and the Weak*, suggests that in marriage there is no distinction between the strong partner and the weak one. Both are involved in a power struggle, but the weak partner uses different weapons. The strong person may be demanding, nagging, and aggressive while the weak person may sulk, withdraw, behave irresponsibly, or even resort to illness or threats of suicide. But all of these modes of behavior are actually attempts to dominate the other person in the power play.[1]

Fritz Perls, in a talk in San Francisco, described the power play in terms of the top-dog/under-dog split and how it works. He said, "The characters differ somewhat, but they have certain structures in common. The top dog usually is righteous, he always knows best. The top dog is the bully and works with [the phrases] 'You should' and 'You should not.' The top dog threatens: 'If you don't, there will be a catastrophe, such as you won't be loved. You won't go to heaven. You will die.' The under dog has no power. The under dog talks like this: 'I try my best. I try again and again. I can't help it if I fail. I can't help it if I forgot your birthday. I have such good intentions.' The under dog is cunning. Both top dog and under dog strive for control like every parent and every child. They strive to get each other under control."

Our Innate Lust for Power

In understanding the person-to-person power game, it is important to separate the lust for power and dominance from the act of actually doing violence to another person. The desire to dominate and have power over another does not mean necessarily that you would misuse or violate him or her in any way. Power seems to be an end in itself.

Konrad Lorenz, in a recent *Psychology Today* article, draws a clear distinction between aggression and violence: "If you put together two little boys, two fish of one species, two roosters, two monkeys, they will behave exactly as Mark Twain describes a meeting between Tom Sawyer and a new boy. The first words Tom says are, 'I can lick you' and the inevitable fight ends just as soon as one boy hollers, 'Nuff!' It is not a drive to kill another person, but the drive to lick him into submission. It has to do with rank, order, or territory and not with a killing instinct. In only two species does fighting between two rivals continue to the death of one adversary: one species of lizard and the Indian elephant. In territorial fights only the loon, a water bird, actually kills a fellow bird in defense of its territory. The scarcity of such examples shows how rare this behavior is."[2]

This seems to be true for people as well. We have an innate need to be aggressive and to dominate with whatever tools, games, or methods are available and suit our purposes. And this same need certainly emerges in our involvement with groups of people, irrespective of whether the group is a service club, a lodge, or a church organization. In fact, the way we handle power and authority largely determines our role and influence within the group.

Perhaps the small group movement within the Christian community has flourished because participants are provided with a means for exerting more direct power. We are weary of getting lost in large groups or organizations where our voice is either not heard or is minimally effective. On the other hand, we can function in small ad hoc groups and see the results of our efforts. Our influence is felt; here we make a difference.

It is true, however, that people in groups, from an army to a lynch mob, often behave in ways which would be unthinkable for them individually. As a case in point, Konrad Lorenz points out how a declaration of war can change a gentle civilian into a fierce killer: "I believe that the success of national socialism was a symptom of a dearth of real ideals. . . . Genetically perfect, decent, good young men create an adversary just in order to be collectively enthusiastic in fighting him. That is the Nazi spirit. . . . The success of Hitler in Germany is evidence of the danger that arises when there are no real ideals to embrace.

"The collective militant enthusiasm which is the prerequisite for war is also the prerequisite for all higher human endeavor. Without the instinct of collective enthusiasm man is an emotional cripple. He cannot get involved in anything. One must educate people so that collective enthusiasm is not misdirected."[3]

Our relationship to power and authority usually determines the type of group in which we are most comfortable. A number of theories have been suggested in recent years to explain the various dynamics taking place in small groups. One suggests that most groups generally swing between two polarities: their task function and their feeling function. While it is true that most groups have a particular job to accomplish, one hopes with speed and efficiency, these same people also have a need to feel included and supported. Groups can opt for one of two classic methods of communication; the star method or the circle method. In the "star method" communication proceeds from all members of the group to the leader or authority figure, who listens, reacts and gives orders. Obviously, group members who have trouble with authority figures will be somewhat frustrated with this method. The "circle method" has no center. Everyone is heard and decisions emerge from some kind of consensus. While this gives each member a chance to exercise power, it is certainly less efficient from a task-oriented point of view.

Nothing has been more helpful to me in understanding the power struggle in groups than my experience at a Tavistock Institute in human relations. The Tavistock approach, the work of British psychoanalyst Wilfred Bion, along with A. K. Rice, is based on theories from Bion's experience in small groups conducted during and after World War II. The Tavistock study group provides a climate in which one can see the development of each individual's fantasies about authority figures and, in particular, the authority figure in that group.

The study group leader or consultant provides boundaries for the group by being punctual, by being formally attired and by staying in character throughout the course of the group, commenting only occasionally and merely as an uninvolved observer. The members of the group, because they invest him with authority, begin to follow his example and to perceive his behavior as coercing theirs.

My group consisted of all kinds of people—army generals, clinical psychiatrists, social workers, and some radical leftists. Some were visibly trying to woo or win the consultant; others were hostile, assuming that he was trying to do something destructive or trying to manipulate them. The rest ignored the leader, refusing even to react, and allied themselves instead with other members of the group in some kind of bid for leadership.

There are specific lessons to be learned from all of this. In every group the participants invest the person acting as the leader with certain powers. All the participants have their own fantasies about the powers of the leader which come from early associations with authority figures. We tend to place all leaders in mommy and daddy roles. If we have rebelled against mommy and daddy, anyone in authority is likely to be challenged. If not, we usually accept authority with good feelings. It is apparent that we all tend to use authority figures in some way to gratify our own particular needs or to reinforce our basic assumptions.

Power and Responsibility

The implications of power are enormous, whether that power is actual—invested automatically in those persons filling particular roles or offices (i.e., the President, the Pope, on down to the schoolteacher)—or whether it is power transferred to any person in an authority role. Most people involved in moving and motivating others—teachers, pastors, politicians, for example—have this kind of role-model power.

Dr. Stanley Milgram conducted a fascinating experiment at Yale to attempt to prove that such widely divergent phenomena as the conduct of the German people under the Nazis or the actions of seemingly responsible and moral men in the Watergate affairs can be explained on the basis of how most people relate to power.

In the experiment two people are told they are part of a study to determine the effects of punishment on learning. One is designated as a teacher and the other is the learner. The learner is positioned in an electrically wired chair, and the teacher is seated before an enormous instrument panel which has thirty switches labeled with voltages ranging from fifteen to four hundred and fifty. In addition to the voltage designations, the switches also bear labels describing shock intensities such as slight, moderate, strong, very strong, intense, extreme, and dangerous. He is told that throwing the switches will transmit an electrical shock to the learner's chair. With everyone in place, Milgram then proceeds to give the learner a word association test. In the meantime the teacher has been instructed to throw the lowest voltage switch for the first incorrect answer and then to increase the shock intensity with each successive mistake.

Milgram describes his experiment this way: "The teacher is a genuinely naïve subject who has come to the laboratory for the experiment. The learner, or victim, is actually an actor who receives no shock at all. The point of the experiment is to see how far a person will proceed in a concrete and measurable situation in which he is ordered to inflict increasing pain on a protesting victim.

"Conflict arises when the man receiving the shock begins to show that he is experiencing discomfort. At seventy-five volts, he grunts; at one hundred twenty-five volts, he complains loudly; at one hundred and fifty, he demands to be released from the experiment. As the voltage increases, his protests become more vehement and emotional. At two hundred and eighty-five volts, his response can be described only as an agonized scream. So thereafter he makes no sound at all."

Of the forty subjects in the first experiment, twenty-five obeyed the experimenter right up to the most powerful shock available. According to Milgram, very few of the subjects seemed to take pleasure in inflicting pain. And those who showed only a small amount of tension or pressure heaved sighs of relief, mopped their brows, rubbed their fingers over their eyes, or nervously fumbled cigarettes when the experiment ended. Several of the subjects tried to halt the experiment but subsequently continued because of the experimenter's firmness and his assurance that he would take responsibility for such things as heart attacks or serious injuries.

"Many of the people were in some sense against what they did to the learner, and many protested even while they obeyed," adds Milgram. But the experiment was carried out in such a way that in order to quit the subject must flatly defy the experimenter. Rather than do that, Milgram says, most of them just went along.[4]

What is it that makes ordinary people follow orders they consider distasteful or even immoral? A critical shift in responsibility takes place when the person sees himself merely as an instrument for carrying out another person's wishes. This is the very heart of obedience carried to its extreme. Morality takes a whole different focus when obedience is in itself a higher good than ethical or humane action. Thus we have German war criminals maintaining they were merely carrying out orders or Watergate defendants insisting they were simply acting in loyalty to their party or their chief. Their actions can be explained only on the basis of the way people relate to orders from those in authority, in whom they have invested seemingly unlimited power.

The Power of the Will

But perhaps the power we most need to understand and explore in our search for meaning and wholeness is the power that each person has over his own life. One of the most interesting revolutions in modern psychiatry and psychology is the rediscovery of the human will. The power that I have over myself has been minimized in the past as we have been viewed as victims of our environment, our unconscious, and our conditioning. Dr. Aubert of Burrswood says, "Conventional psychiatry under the influence of the behaviorist and Freudian schools has reduced the area of man's free will almost to nothing, making him little more than the helpless victim of instinctual drives, conditioned reflexes, heredity, environment, physiology, and so on."

The Italian psychiatrist Roberto Assagioli asserts that the nonrecognition of the human will is the scandal of modern psychology. And William Glasser, discussing Reality Therapy with a group of us in Baltimore, pointed out that we can have choices about the direction of our lives. The problem is that so often we choose to pretend that we do not. He said, "There is nothing that undercuts effective living more than excuses. If you want to try something, start on Monday and try to live just five days of your life without excusing anything you do. Just live a whole week without excusing anything. If you're late and people ask what happened, just say, 'I'm late because I am incompetent.' There is no other reason, so you may as well tell the truth. You'll only say that once and you won't be late for a long, long time after that. If someone asks, 'Why didn't you do it?' Say, 'Because I didn't want to' if that is the truth. But most of the things people are asking you about you've got control over. And if it isn't exercised, say that you're incompetent, you're lazy."

This power over self can perhaps be the most creative use of power. As I see it, the power that others use to manipulate me in relationships or the powers exerted on us through groups can be overcome by the power we exercise over ourselves.

I can choose to be happy. No one can take that right away from me. I am responsible for myself. And what is wrong with me as well as what is right with me is the result of my own choices. And, I believe that God can be a participant in those choices. Feeling that we are loved and have worth gives us courage to live in this radically courageous way.

Chapter 5

Your Capacity to Change

Karl Marx once said, "If you want to understand the structure of the world, try to change it." I'm convinced this is true for people as well. In fact, our attitude toward change, in my opinion, can be an accurate measure of our growth toward wholeness.

Far too many of us, unfortunately, are locked into set patterns of thinking and living. We resist change vigorously, satisfied with the comfortable rigidity of our stale routines.

And yet we know that life is movement, not a static position. Arnold Toynbee once defined civilization as "a movement and not a condition; a voyage, not a harbor." To live is to act . . . to do . . . to be. Inactivity produces atrophy, stagnation and death. Medically speaking, movement and activity are signs that the patient is on the way to recovery.

Our Instinctive Resistance to Change

Some years ago John Gardner, in his remarkable little book *Self Renewal*, suggested that the capacity for self-renewal—another name for constructive change—is the most vital single ingredient in the survival of an individual, an organization, a nation, or a civilization.[1] But, tragically, far too often the Christian church has been a powerful change-resisting agent. The gospel of Jesus Christ has been used to fight change and to keep things as they are. In the past the Bible has been cited as a defense for slavery and an excuse for the second-class status of women. It has been quoted to justify those opposing scientific advances of all sorts. What a perversion of God's true nature and plan. It seems to me that a far more accurate picture of God's purpose for us is found in Isaiah 43:18–19: "Cease to dwell on days gone by and to brood over past history. Here and now I will do a new thing; this moment it will break from the bud. Can you not perceive it?" (NEB).

To me the very heart of the nature of God is that he initiates change. It is true that he is an unchanging God whose nature and purpose are stable, but as he interacts in the world of men, he is always bringing forth a new thing, guiding and leading those who believe in him and respond to him. In fact, the unchanging God is the initiator of change.

But there's even a paradox here, because even the most adventuresome of us—those of us who are the least committed to and defensive of the past—still fear change. I've read that people who have been faced with freezing to death in the snow experience a cozy warm feeling that seduces them into inactivity. But to survive, a person must shake off this wonderful, comfortable feeling which leads to death and start to act by changing position frequently, by forcing activity.

To stay alive during long exposure to freezing conditions, one has to go against instinctive feelings. To think the way we always have, to act in old patterns is nonthreatening and comfortable, but it lulls us toward a frightening death of the soul. To stay alive we must be people on the move, alert to the exciting opportunities of change.

An Environment for Change

Surely one of the most hazardous aspects of marriage is that it represents change in enormous and sudden proportions. Twenty-five years ago when my wife, Hazel, and I were married, it was assumed that parenthood was the next step whether we were ready for it or not. We believed that parenthood cemented and enriched a marriage and that childless couples were somewhat incomplete. But recently in Ann Arbor, Michigan, a team of research experts came up with a report that explodes that very popular myth. According to their studies, the happiest married couples are those without children. Further, they have concluded that we have been largely misled about the pain and sorrow associated with that time when children leave home and lead lives of their own. The research team said, "The time of the empty nest turns out to be a time of fulfillment."

To have children is to be constantly subject to the strain and stress of change. Raising children means living with uncertainty. Their health may break down, or their behavior may cause you embarrassment. Even society may give you unpleasant feedback about your children, from the kindergarten teacher to a policeman on the narcotics squad.

On the other hand, while a childless environment may seem to be more trouble-free and in a sense happier, a home that is charged with the daily interaction of children is a place where change is a must and where learning and growth are facilitated. Change for most of us does not feel good, but it is essential to the growth which is a requirement of wholeness.

Dimensions of Change

At a seminar at the University of Massachusetts, I saw a rather graphic demonstration of our basic attitude toward change. Announcing that he was going to test our powers of observation, our instructor, Dr. Ken Blanchard, had us pair off by twos and carefully observe each other. Then, turning back to back, we were each to make ten changes in our appearance. Next, we were to reexamine the other person and try to discover what changes he or she had made.

After completing this part of the exercise, Blanchard asked, "How many of you in making changes took things off and how many added things?" In the room of several hundred people almost all of us made changes by removing something: watches, glasses, sweaters, earrings, shoes, socks, pens, pencils, etc. Very few of us added anything. From this, the conclusion was neatly drawn that most of us have an inborn fear of change because we think it will cause us to lose something. To conquer that inborn feeling, we must somehow reprogram ourselves to feel that change means gaining and growing.

Blanchard then talked about four dimensions of change to which we are equally resistant. The first is a *knowledge* change. We change because we come to know more about a person, subject, situation, approach, or strategy. Schools major in this kind of change. And perhaps for most people, change at this level is the least threatening and the most appealing.

Second, there is *attitudinal* change. This level of change involves the emotions. People feel strongly about a certain position, precept, or approach and resist any attempts to change those attitudes.

The third level of change is *behavioral* change. This means that in spite of how we feel, in spite of our fears, reluctance, or doubts, we are trying to change our behavior. And as difficult as behavioral change is, in my opinion, it is less difficult than attitudinal change. Perhaps this is because we have less control over our emotions, feelings, and attitudes than we do over our behavior. If we can start with behavioral changes—do something differently, approach a problem with more integrity, perform deliberate acts to express love and concern—perhaps an attitude change will result. There is actually strong psychological and historical evidence to prove that when behavior changes, attitudes change. The civil rights legislation of the past decades is just one instance of this. By changing our national behavior, our national attitudes are slowly but surely beginning to change.

The fourth level of change was *organizational* change—a change in group behavior. This is both complex and threatening. When a familiar organization to which we belong, such as a church, civic group, union, social or service club, decides to change its rules, goals, membership, or financial policies, it is usually upsetting to those of us who did not initiate the change. Most of us derive a great deal of security from the groups we belong to, and any attempt to change those groups represents a threat to our security pattern and our way of life.

Conversion and Change

One of the great American psychologists, William James, was fascinated with the subject of change and with the conversion experience in particular. He believed radical change was not only possible but could be documented in many lives. He made a careful study of people who had experienced conversion to find out how change came about. His definition of conversion appears in his book *The Varieties of Religious Experience,* published in 1902, and it is to me a definition of radical change in terms of both behavior and identity. "To be converted . . . is a process, gradual or sudden, by which a self hitherto divided, and consciously wrong, inferior, and unhappy, becomes unified and consciously right, superior, and happy, in consequence of its firmer hold upon religious realities."

After exhaustive research into the lives of many people who had been converted, James found a pattern emerging.

"The steps leading up to the conversion experience are three-fold: effort, passivity, and surrender."

An example from everyday life (one, incidentally, which Frankl uses in logotherapy) can clarify this for us. Suppose you are trying to recall someone's name but you simply cannot think of it. The name is buried in your subconscious and the more you try to grasp it, the more it eludes you. We've all had this experience. Finally, you give up. You forget about it; you surrender. Almost immediately or perhaps just a short time later, it bursts into your consciousness. Apparently, the way to remember a name is to stop trying after you first tried very hard.

So it is with the conversion experience, according to James. If you are pursuing an experience of God with your whole soul, the odds are it will happen only when you give up, surrender, and quit trying. James is quick to say, however, that being able to explain the conversion experience psychologically does not account for the miraculous part God plays in it. To understand the experience does not mean you can duplicate it. Channels and methods by which God touches a life, unlocks the subsconscious, and gives power in a new way cannot be controlled. Nor can this be psychologically induced or manipulated.

The Place of the Will

James wrote all this at the beginning of the twentieth century, and things have changed considerably since then. With the birth and growth of psychoanalysis, the importance of the will in the process of change has been greatly minimized, whether one is a Freudian or a behaviorist, as we said in the last chapter.

But more recently, psychological pioneers have been re-examining the role of the will in change. Roberto Assagioli, founder and developer of Psychosynthesis in Italy, who was quoted earlier, had this to say in an interview just before his death: "I believe the will is the Cinderella of modern psychology. It has been relegated to the kitchen. The Victorian notion that will power could overcome all obstacles was destroyed by Freud's discovery of unconscious motivation. But, unfortunately, this led modern psychology into a deterministic view of man as a bundle of competing forces with no center. This is contrary to every human being's direct experience of himself. At some point, perhaps in a crisis when danger threatens, an awakening occurs in which the individual discovers his will. This revelation that the self and the will are intimately connected can change a person's whole awareness of himself and the world. He sees that he is a living subject, an actor, endowed with the power to choose, to relate, to bring about changes in his own personality, in others, in circumstances. And this awareness leads to a feeling of wholeness, security and joy."

When the interviewer asked Assagioli what techniques he used to develop will power, he said; "One technique is visualizing the 'ideal model.' Picture as vividly as possible how your life would be different if you were in possession of a strong will. Visualize yourself as having attained inner and outer mastery. We also advise performing some 'useless exercises' every day for strengthening self-discipline. If the will is placed in direct opposition to strong feelings or drives it will be overpowered and so we have to create a strategy to achieve the ends we will. Take, for example, a person with an obsessive desire who wills to be rid of his obsession. The more he concentrates on the obsession, the fiercer it grows. But he can withhold his attention and substitute a new interest; he can cultivate a beneficent 'obsession.' Holding new images before the eye tends to produce the reality suggested by the image. This follows from a well-known psychological law: Images or mental pictures and ideas tend to produce the physical conditions and external acts that correspond to them. . . . One very simple technique I use is a series of cards on which are printed evocative words such as: CALM, PATIENCE, BLISS, ENERGY, GOOD-WILL. When these cards are placed around the room they trigger attitudes and call forth the quality they symbolize."[2]

Assagioli's approach may seem simplistic, but I think he is rediscovering an age-old truth. Those who have ridiculed the positive-thinking approach of Coué or Norman Vincent Peale which swept this country twenty years ago may have to reexamine that philosophy. Psychologically it seems to be a valid and sound approach.

The group process and the dynamic of group process provides this 'ideal model' Assagioli speaks of which enables change. I have seen this work dramatically in Christian groups. People have experienced God and been changed because of their desire and need to conform to the group's ideals. This is not necessarily bad. In a positive way, God can use his church as a family of believers to bring about his ends. God's most powerful witness to the world may very well be the small companies of his people who try to live in fellowship with one another in obedience to his will. Those who come in contact with such a group are drawn into it, strengthened tremendously in their faith, and sometimes led to a conversion experience.

Strategies for Change

In talking about strategies of change, Dwight Allen emphasizes the importance of timing. There is a right time when the climate for change is maximum. If we have a gift for sensing this right time, we will have much less difficulty bringing about change. Further, he suggests, in presenting new programs or any course of action which requires change, tell it like it is. In other words, be honest and vulnerable. "Don't try to make things look like something they are not," he cautions. "Don't act as if you have all the answers and know the answers." If we are exploring and probing, largely uncertain about our goals or methods, we should be frank about it. For many kinds of change, especially in the area of education that is Allen's specialty, he feels we don't need to know what our goal is. Knowing our goal may even be counterproductive. In a search for a more adequate way to educate people, we are explorers and adventurers, not those committed to hard and fast goals.

He also indicated that most change takes place through other than the established channels, through alleyways rather than main highways. The changers in any given organization are not usually part of the leadership group. Finally, Allen's strategy of change includes learning to eliminate things. Change means adding but it also means losing. He decries the fact that in the field of education, we take on new courses, new curricula, new approaches but never let go of the old, which have become somehow sacrosanct. This principle applies to personal change as well. In acquiring new skills or learning new approaches, I must eliminate along the way things that no longer have value or have less value. Otherwise my life is overextended and I am frustrated.

For example, the *Better Homes and Garden* type homemaker who decides to write a book or join a little theater group or sell real estate may find her family becoming hostile because meals are skimpy or late and the house is messy. She can explain what is happening and win their understanding and cooperation, or she can learn to live in the tension. If she simply adds her new interest to all the old responsibilities, she may lose the whole ball game. Planned neglect is a must when any person or family or institution wishes to change its goals or add new goals.

While Allen's strategies for change relate understandably to the educational scene of which he is a part, they are surely applicable for organizational changes of all kinds, from small groups to institutions. Since change is inescapable and inevitable, the question to be faced is whether we change enthusiastically and happily or whether we dig our heels in and are brought kicking and screaming into the next experience that life has for us.

Two Kinds of Change: Chosen and Unchosen

It seems to me that all of us experience two basic kinds of change: inevitable change and self-initiated change. Inevitable change occurs simply because we are alive. Friends die; we become ill; we make money or we lose money; wars start; our children grow up, leave home, or disappoint us—all of life is a series of disruptive changes. It's difficult enough to handle positive change that somehow improves our state, but the change that deprives us of what we hold dear is most dreaded and frightening.

I believe there are surprising resources in most people for handling inevitable change. Even people with no declared religious faith or conscious resources of strength somehow manage to handle the blows that life deals out. Surprisingly few people break down emotionally or physically. Most everyone comes through with courage and resiliency.

In 1966 one of the great tragedies of our century happened in Aberfan, Wales, a community of three thousand people. A few minutes before noon on a wet, gray morning, the children of this tiny mining village had just settled down to their lessons in the junior school. Suddenly they heard a loud roar that sounded like a low-flying jet. Actually, it came from a 111-foot mountain of rubbish from the coal mine. Constant rain had turned a mountain of slag waste into a slimy black tidal wave, and it came roaring over the school, engulfing it. The wave of muck suffocated or crushed to death one hundred and sixteen children and twenty-eight adults.

The townspeople were in shock and grief. For a time some of the surviving children were too frightened to go to school or even to leave their homes. Bitter quarrels broke out between parents who had lost a child and those whose children were unscathed, between the Aberfan villagers and the coal mine authorities, between Aberfan and nearby towns. Hysterical symptoms developed in many of the parents who could not vocalize their grief. Some women were unable to visit the grocery store or the hairdresser without the help of some professional worker. But slowly, as people from all over the world pitched in with money and offers of help, some semblance of life came again to Aberfan, and the horror began to fade.

The psychiatrists and social workers who worked in Aberfan during the rehabilitation period have found that apparently the lives of the people have changed for the good. The town is becoming a community of caring people with a sensitivity for personal and community life.

The lesson of Aberfan, for me, is that God has placed astounding resources in human beings. When the very worst strikes us, great good is frequently standing at the threshold. Powerful forces for healing and health and community can be released as we deal with inevitable change.

Self-initiated change, on the other hand, is that change which comes about as the result of choice. We can choose to risk and dare in relationships, in financial or vocational matters, or in causes that affect our neighborhood and world. I believe we need help with this kind of change—the help available through personal relationships and small groups. We can encourage each other to be open to change, to have positive attitudes toward it, to become people who are able to change and to act as change agents for one another in society.

We have overcome the universal basic fear of change when we can welcome the uncertain future with a minimum of reluctance and a maximum of anticipation. When this happens, we are on our way to wholeness. The belief that man can change is essential to our Christian faith. In the Judeo-Christian tradition, God is the creator, the very initiator of change.

A good question to ask ourselves at this point is, Am I ready to change? Do I need to change? In *I'm OK—You're OK*, Thomas Harris claims that we are ready to change first of all when we are unhappy with the situation as it is and want to change—in other words, when to stay as we are is more painful than change. Next, we are ready to change when we are at the point of despair. Change is an option, for instance, for the person who is tired of his alcoholism or the person suffering depression or the person whose marriage is dissolving. Finally, change is often brought about at the "eureka" stage. This can happen at a religious meeting or a transactional analysis workshop or by meeting someone we can identify with who says he has changed.

Learning comes best by models. Abraham, the patriarch, is one of our primary models for change. By choice he left his home and friends and business and country and culture and began a search in strange places for what he believed was God's destiny for him and for the spiritual nation to follow. He failed, he flinched, he doubted, he lied—but he never went home. Change and uncertainty were his constant companions—*by choice*. The Bible calls Abraham the father of the faithful because of his ability to choose change in response to God's leading.

Somehow linked to life and a belief in God is the ability to face head-on the universal fear of change, to meet the inevitable changes that come with courage and resources, and to move out in creative ways to lose old images and old patterns and to embrace a self-initiated change.

Chapter 6

Dare to Be Different

Paul Tournier's Medicine of the Whole Person is based on his belief in the uniqueness of individuals. In a conversation one day we were reflecting on how two people can have the same experience and yet be affected so differently. He believes there is just no way to predict how any person will handle a given set of circumstances. For example, two of his patients are women who were sexually assaulted by their fathers when they were children. One became ill and incapable of sexual relations. The other has made a healthy adjustment and enjoys a normal sex life.

The Affective Climate

Tournier reports further that while some people get sick from fear, others are stimulated by it; some become stronger with abuse, while others are destroyed by it. The determining factor seems to be internal rather than external because responses are difficult to control or manipulate consciously.

Those determining factors have very early origins, according to Dr. Tournier. In *The Naming of Persons,* he claims our capacity for self-acceptance is shaped by the acceptance we receive beginning in infanthood. When that little person is named, the name itself implies a mysterious and unknown future beyond anything the parents can imagine. If the mother sees the infant as an object of her love, utterly dependent on her and existing to satisfy her, the "affective climate" is damaging. Only if the child is accepted as a unique human being who exists in himself and not to satisfy the parents can he eventually grow into self-acceptance and develop the ability to give and receive love.[1]

As Tournier has described, infants born to be unique are often stunted by parents who have an unhealthy need for them and their love. When other loves have failed us or we have disappointed ourselves, we tend to make these new human beings extensions of our own egos. They exist to make *us* feel important. Their own uniqueness and personhood is not affirmed.

Feelings and Dignity

In a workshop led by *I'm OK—You're OK* authors Tom and Amy Harris, Amy probed some of the things we have learned about our feelings from our parents. For example, when a small child bursts into the house screaming, "It hurts, it hurts," the conditioned response of many parents is, "Stop crying. It doesn't hurt." With that, the child says to himself, "Gee, that's funny. I thought it hurt." He immediately begins to distrust his own feelings and to believe the feelings of the parent.

The next day, the child in a fit of anger may say, "I hate Billy. He's nasty." "You don't hate Billy," his mother replies, "You love Billy. He's your brother." Again the child computes this: "Gee, I thought I hated Billy but I guess I don't."

You see how this works? The authentic feelings of the child begin to be distrusted if the parent does not honor them. Now we don't set out deliberately to confuse and scar our children, but it is still true that many of us are suffering now because of those simple, childhood feelings that were not accepted and taken seriously. When parents impose what they consider "right" feelings, the child is then robbed of his own uniqueness. And this can lead to complicated problems later which may not be resolved without therapeutic help.

When we are not taken seriously about our feelings or our needs, we suffer the loss of our sense of uniqueness. And to lose our uniqueness is to lose our dignity. Thomas Szasz, in speaking to a graduating class of doctors, asserted that many prospective patients value their dignity above their health and even their life.

We are now coming to a reawakening of the truth that dignity of the person is of primary importance. Today's educators are beginning to stress the need for dignity. Arthur Combs, at the University of Florida, claims that, in the past, schools have often violated the dignity of students, and as a result, the students have felt both joyless and worthless. And even the armed services are beginning to take seriously the uniqueness of their recruits and their need for dignity. Recruitment posters suggest that the Army will join you. The subtle idea comes across that they will meet you where you are, with the lifestyle you presently enjoy, with the freedom to do your own thing in a private room.

Non-Conformity: A New Message for the Church

Now to carry this a step further, I believe that we are unique in our capacity for creativity. While in London a while ago I heard Michael Baughen, the vicar of All Saints Church, make this comment in his sermon: "We are not like the animals, because animals cannot create. All animals can do is use and consume and be themselves. Only man being made in the image of God can create. Not *ex nihilo* as

God can, but, nevertheless, man builds buildings and bridges, writes poems and symphonies and even splits atoms. Man creates, and when we are in God's plan we are meant to be like our Creator."

In the twentieth century we have seen the Christian church begin to revamp its home and foreign missionary programs to honor and include the uniqueness of people. In the heart of London, Cliff and Monica Hill direct the Eastham Community Renewal Project—one of the most effective urban renewal programs I've seen. A combination of clergy and lay volunteers from many different denominations are involved in a strategy for reclaiming churches no longer able to maintain their buildings in the inner city. Outlining their strategy, Clifford Hill says, "First, analyze the social structure of the community. Get to know people; where they are from, what their ethnic backgrounds are, their culture, their social customs, family traditions, so you know the people to whom you are going to relate. You cannot relate to people, build up relationships with them, and help them renew relationships with God if you do not understand them. It goes without saying that you must respect their culture, their traditions, and their social customs, and you must respect them as people. This is essential for the Christian. We don't go in there with this kind of superior, patronizing attitude that says we're going to change you, brother, because we've got what it takes and you haven't."

To understand the scope of what Cliff is saying, it's important to know that the people who live in and around the Eastham Renewal Project come from every major country in the world and represent literally every major religion. Cliff and his associates believe that people can be reached and helped and even evangelized if one honors their uniqueness culturally, religiously, and psychologically. And it seems to be working, because churches that formerly housed just a handful of people for an hour on Sunday are now filled to capacity for each service, and the buildings are used seven days a week.

The Pressure to Conform

But while both the psychological and religious worlds are beginning to take our differences seriously, there is also a subtle and relentless pressure on us to conform. This is exerted by parents, friends, churches, traditions, and society as a whole. There is so much about our cultural patterns that pushes us toward conformity. Conformity, pressure to conform, must be resisted vigorously if we are to find wholeness. "Conforming" robs us of our uniqueness, our spiritual and emotional wholeness, and perhaps our very soul. Even in our attempts to deliberately rebel and be a nonconformist, we find ourselves conforming to the other nonconformists. There seems to be no hiding place.

The forces that work to make us conform are overwhelming, from the organizational or social structures we find ourselves in (schools, churches, families, our peers, our neighborhood) to the more subtle value-communication forces that work through television, newspapers, magazines, movies, or best-selling novels. Perhaps the best defense against the restrictiveness of conformity is to be actively engaged in the search for our uniqueness, and it seems to me there are at least three key steps in that search: getting in touch with our feelings, attempting honest relationships in the present, discovering and affirming our unique and particular gifts.

Dealing with Our Unique Feelings

To become a whole person I must be in touch with my feelings. In the past we have often minimized the importance of our feelings, and even today, we are somewhat ashamed to confess an illness considered largely psychosomatic. But the relationship between emotions and physical well-being is a well-established fact. Most of us are aware through personal experience that feelings of embarrassment, excitement, anger, or fear are accompanied by tangible physical changes. Phrases like "being burned up with resentment" or "eaten up with self-pity" are in themselves descriptive of what is actually happening to us physically as a result of these emotions. Dr. Aubert of Burrswood Clinic says, "Is a doctor to concern himself with such things as anger, resentment, bitterness, and self-pity? If they are making his patient ill as they often do, then he must. But how many medical schools obsessed with technology pay attention to these things, even where psychosomatic medicine is recognized as a respectable specialty?"

An article in a recent issue of *The Journal of the American Medical Association* estimates that at least half of each doctor's patients have ailments that are either entirely emotional or that have emotional overtones. (Most doctors I know feel that the figure is closer to 90 percent.) Some doctors refer to them as "the worried well." They are the casualties of the pace of modern life.

I strongly believe that paramedical groups and lay groups within the church have tremendous potential for healing and helping people like this. Dealing with our feelings seems to be one of our most basic problems, but unfortunately, medical doctors—at least many of them—do not seem to have the time or inclination to help in this area.

Probing our feelings in conversations with another person or with a small group is usually helpful. For example, expressing my feelings about myself, my spouse, my children, my boss, or my friends can be a first step toward a better handling of them. In reality, our attitude toward particular difficulties and hurts is far more important than the actual circumstances. Our feelings are determined by our attitudes, and, happily, we do have control over those attitudes.

Dr. Aubert validates this idea: "Most of us have met men and women whose suffering has made them more humble, more tolerant, more sympathetic, and less concerned with their own affairs. There are those on the other hand for whom everything in life has been easy who tend to be egocentric, immature, and lacking in feeling for others. It is our attitude to our trials and tribulations that is all-important."

Feelings can be controlled far more than we have previously believed, and they can be harnessed for creative purposes. At an *I'm OK—You're OK* workshop in Sacramento, California, Mrs. Harris explained this in a rather intriguing way during a discussion of why people cry. She outlined three reasons: Tears may be caused by playing "old tapes"—deeply buried parental injuctions from childhood. Then, tears may be a means of blackmail, in which the weeper attempts to manipulate or influence others through their tears. Finally, tears can indicate a release of feeling after times of intimacy or joy. The important thing is never to be intimidated by tears, even our own, in the effort to help people get in touch with their feelings.

Gestalt therapy claims that we are able to exert a great deal of control over feelings of pain, depression, and anger. There seems ample indication that emotions are subject to our wills to a great extent. There is a theory that women tend to live longer than men because they are more free to cry or scream or express affection. If this is true, then men can reverse the deadly effects of their emotional constipation by choosing to deal with their feelings more openly. Gestalt therapy insists that we face the fact that we are not victims. We have made a deliberate choice not to own our feelings. When I realize that I can control my emotions consciously, I am on the way to wholeness in the feelings part of my life.

Creative Relationships

Another important means of discovering our uniqueness is through honest relationships with the significant people in our lives. One of the primary ways in which I can move toward a better self-understanding is through seeing myself reflected in the eyes of others. They mirror who I am. And at an even deeper level, relationships can be a means of delivering me from a prison of dishonesty or from crippling conformity. In a relationship of love and trust and acceptance, it becomes difficult to be dishonest. (In the same way, the other person can be the means of discovering or affirming gifts and talents I may never have recognized.) My relationships with those around me can contribute to my life or add an imprisoning, dehumanizing, conforming dimension.

Eric Berne taught us all a lot about relationships in his book *Games People Play*. Frequently we play "games" which allow imprisoning relationships to continue. Games can include such chosen roles as "poor me," ". . . but all I did was . . . ," "can't you ever do anything right," or "shape up or I'll leave you." In an exercise at the Harris Institute, the roles we choose to play in all of the various games that Eric Berne describes have been reduced to three basic ones—the victim, the persecutor, and the rescuer. Your life script determines in different situations which role you will choose for yourself. You may feel that you are being victimized or persecuted. Perhaps you are the one who has a need to rescue the victims of unhappy situations. Or you may be the persecutor who enjoys manipulating and using others. Once I recognize that I am choosing one of these roles in a relationship, and possibly in many relationships, then I can begin to examine the merits of the role itself and I can choose to play it or not. Instead of allowing myself to get trapped in my usual role, I can opt for more honest relationships, based on "game-free" friendship.

The importance of honesty within relationships certainly applies in marriage. William Shutz, in a workshop at the University of Maryland, comments: "When one person is hiding something, the marriage deteriorates. If there is something you're covering up, you can't afford to be spontaneous. You must be contained and you must have everything under control and you must censor everything that comes out because you might give yourself away. It's a pleasure to get out of the house because you somehow feel a little freer. And when you approach the house you know something is happening to you—your body is beginning to tighten up and you're getting much more constricted. . . . A couple [in a counseling situation] will come in saying the marriage is dull, not knowing that the dullness is related to all the withholding. The more open they can both be, the more they are really there for each other and the more total and complete the relationship can be."

The Discovery of Gifts

A third stop in our search for uniqueness, it seems to me, is to discover and use the special gifts we have. Here, I am separating gifts from our skills or talents simply because skills are learned, acquired, or developed, while gifts are innate. However, once discovered, our particular gifts can be encouraged and expanded, but they are a unique and integral part of one's self.

One day a woman asked of Marcel Proust, the great French poet, "Mr. Proust, is it hard to write poetry?" "Madam," he responded, "If it isn't easy, it's impossible." Like the gift for poetry, these innate gifts are a natural part of all of us and are an expression of our uniqueness. All too often we tend to think of only poets or artists or musicians or writers as being gifted, but all of us are gifted in some way that can bring joy, worth, and freedom to ourselves and to others.

In *Harper's* magazine, I came across the story of a housewife who was using her gifts to create newness in her environment. Margot Moes-Hunt, who lives in Brooklyn Heights, wrote: "For a long time after my marriage was in trouble, I went through agonizing days of self-doubt and depression. With two children under four years old, there was no way for me to get out of the house for a change, so I decided to change the house I was in. I took one room at a time and attacked it with a furious impromptu redecorating fervor. First I settled on some color combination that pleased me—blue, mauve, and lots of white, or brown and green. And then I'd change everything around.

"I dyed my towels blue and then green and then orange. Then I sewed them up double and made them into pillows by stuffing them with blankets or old clothes. Sheets followed the same process, and my quilts have at one time or another been rugs, table cloths, and curtains.

"I painted the shutters in several gradations of color. I filled the fireplace with white stones gathered over the years on many beaches and topped them with small plants under a grow light. It all seems very simple, but it never failed to cheer me up because I forced myself to create something from nothing every day."[2]

Margot Moes-Hunt is an artist in her own way, as she uses her gifts to change her world. While we can't all change our surroundings with that same artistic inventiveness, we can be similarly creative in using the gifts we have in our jobs, hobbies or situations.

In an article in *Saturday Review-World*, Arthur Mandell, a psychologist, discussed using one's particular gifts to the best advantage in the game of football. He maintains that offensive football players like structure and discipline. They tend to be conservative as people and like to maintain the status quo. This makes it easy for them to enjoy the repetitious practice of well-planned and well-executed plays.

On the other hand, defensive players are just as firm in their abhorrence of structure. Their attitudes, their behavior and their lifestyles seem to bear this out. They instinctively enjoy challenging the rules or regulations put forward by anybody. Coaches find defensive players much more difficult to manage than their offensive teammates.

The conclusions from Mandell's study are obvious. Making a proper match between player and position is necessary not only for team success but for personal happiness. Players working in the wrong position are uneasy and attempt to compensate for their uneasiness. Like the rest of us, they become demoralized and lose effectiveness when they aren't in the right place, doing what comes naturally. Dr. Mandell's conviction that success in football requires playing the position that corresponds best with one's personality gifts is appropriate for the rest of us as well. We need to find the place where our gifts can best be used.

According to Kenneth Waites, a Methodist District Superintendent in Newcastle, England, whom I talked with, the calling forth of gifts at the time of the Wesleyan revival brought social healing on a national scale. He claims that the present British Labor Movement actually emerged from the Wesleyan revival. At Methodist class meetings people were converted, taught to read (beginning with the Scriptures), encouraged to speak in public to bear witness for Christ. When these same people began to speak about intolerable labor conditions, many were elected by their peers and sent to Parliament. To this day many of the strongest leaders in the Labor Movement in England are Methodists, and they are a reminder of a time when the leadership for the original Labor Movement was trained in class meetings by John Wesley.

There were many forces at work to make you and me the unique people we are now—our genetic background, our upbringing (or affective climate, as Tournier describes it), our feelings, our relationships, our gifts. Affirming and exploring that uniqueness is an integral part of being whole. I live on an island world famous for its sea shells. Any random walk on the beach reveals to me all over again God's infinite creativity. It seems to me that only as he is able to help us become the one of a kind creation we are meant to be can we ultimately fit into the cosmic jigsaw puzzle that he is working out.

Chapter 7

To Live Is to Risk

As far as I know, Homer Dodge is the world's only eighty-five-year-old white-water canoeist. He is also President Emeritus of Norwich University in Vermont, a writer, explorer, cartographer, adventurer, and ecologist. Dodge started canoeing at age five as a remedial exercise for a broken arm. By age ten he was paddling on the St. Lawrence River as far as he could go in one day. At sixty-nine Dodge became the only person since the time of the early fur traders to run the dangerous Long Salt Rapids before the St. Lawrence Seaway removed them forever. When asked the secret of this obviously successful and fulfilling life, Dodge said, "If you want to have interesting experiences, put yourself where they can happen." Dodge was highlighting one of the vital ingredients of any fulfilling life—the capacity to choose risk.

Courting Risk

Dr. T. Glynn Williams, Associate Director of the Maryland Psychiatric Research Center, told me recently that he doesn't believe man was created to be safe, and if there is no risk and danger in his life, he will create it. He sees this as a constructive urge rather than a destructive one. The need for danger and risk is universal to all of mankind—African bushmen, Australian aborigines, or urban dwellers in Brooklyn. Deprived of danger, man has a deep inner need to create some, or, like Homer Dodge, to put himself where "interesting things" can happen.

If the need for risk indicates health, then the need for safety, at least an inordinate need for safety, is an indication of mental illness. In *Journey Out of Nowhere,* Nancy Covert Smith describes her own mental breakdown.[1] A good church member and a professing Christian, she gets to the point where she must enter a mental hospital. While there she comes to a realization that the doors are locked not primarily to keep the inmates in, but to keep the world out. She attributes 50 to 60 percent of the healing process which took place during her confinement to the fact that the world is kept outside locked doors. Part of mental illness then is an overwhelming and unnatural need to be safe. But to live in the real world of people and relationships is obviously risky.

"I never promised you a rose garden" was an expression that caught on a while back. It was used to describe what life is like today and the cost of most primary relationships. Some churches present the Christian life as a haven from tribulation, rejection, and failure, but the biblical truth is that Jesus never promised his followers a "rose garden." He never promised any of us that he would keep us from pain and suffering. Rather he promises us that we will experience trouble, but we have his assurance, "Lo, I am with you always even unto the end of the world."

Throughout all of history, Christians of great commitment have courted and encouraged risk in their own lives. Rupert Mayer, a German Jesuit priest and chaplain in the First World War, is described by Philip Caraman: "There was nothing charismatic in his spiritual life, but he had abundant and controlled charity. His features were rugged and handsome, his face heavily lined; his eyes possessed a disconcerting penetration. He spoke softly, his courtesy was unassumingly natural, his expression calm but indicative of continuous suffering, both physical (for he was lame) and spiritual (for he fought a lonely battle against evil). Unmistakably his friends were conscious of being confronted with a saint. At the height of Nazi power he preached bravely against the irreligion of the regime; he refused to be silenced, returning always to the defense of the conscientious rights of Catholic, Lutheran and Jew. When Hitler, whom he had known as a youthful private and an underground agitator, sent him a telegram of congratulations on his priestly jubilee, he tore up the paper in the pulpit before his congregation. With Pastor Niemöller, he became a symbol of resistance to a resurgent barbarism. Fearlessly he condemned blasphemous cartoons —it was the time German bookshops displayed prints depicting the Nazi Führer standing on a wooden table in a Munich beer cellar addressing his spellbound disciples, with the caption below, '*Am Anfang war das Wort*' ('In the beginning was the word'). Wherever he proposed to preach, though no public notice was given, hundreds were turned away from the crowded church. In and out of concentration camps this was his life for more than ten years. Today he is buried in the Burgersall Kirche in Munich. The stream of pilgrims there is incessant from morning until night."[2]

Intuitively, all of us recognize that someone who risks greatly for his beliefs and values is an authentic person worthy of admiration. Secretly, we all wish to be people like that, who have the courage to risk for the things we believe in. Keith Miller brings this insight to his counseling. This Episcopal layman and author is one of the most gifted counselors I know. He compares counseling to helping people cross a stream. They've been standing on the bank and can see just one rock. He encourages them to get out on that rock and then perhaps from that perspective they will see another just below the surface, and then another until they've made it across. I asked him one time what happens to people who stumble and fall into the stream during the course of counseling. He responded that it's better to fall in than to stand on the bank wishing for a way to get across. You may even find that the stream is not as deep as you feared.

Taking that first step is risky because it may be the beginning of self-knowledge, and the great risk for any man, according to Keith, is to find the truth about himself. In his own words, "Often I want to know the truth about myself, but I'm afraid to find it out for fear that it will be something I can't handle. . . . To risk finding out who I am—to enter into dialogue with a group or a counselor or just with myself is a kind of creative risk-taking that points the way to wholeness or self-actualization."

Overcoming Fear

The obvious block to a creative kind of risky living is fear. My own attitude toward fear keeps me at times from behaving responsibly. I happen to have, for example, a very low threshold of pain in my teeth, and I dread going to the dentist. From the moment I make a dental appointment I begin to suffer a peculiar kind of torture in anticipation of those minutes in the dentist's chair. I'm sure my fear of the pain has prevented me many times from receiving prompt dental help. But the fear itself has been crippling. The actual pain that I've experienced in the dentist's chair is very real, but also very brief. But my fear of going has kept me from being at my best for hundreds of hours and has had its own peculiar effect on my life.

The great rallying cry of President Franklin Delano Roosevelt as he took office in 1932 in the heart of the Great Depression was, "We have nothing to fear but fear itself." This is an astute observation; fear must be dealt with as an entity in its own right. In a recent book entitled *The Fearful Void,* Geoffrey Moorhouse tells of his attempt to deal with the fear of fear. It is a candid account of a British journalist's unsuccessful attempt to make the first solo crossing of the Sahara Desert by camel from the Atlantic to the Nile. Moorhouse knew from the start that his real reason for undertaking this unique adventure was to conquer his own fear of fear. On an earlier occasion he had flown over the vast Sahara, and the sheer enormity and desolation of the wasteland below had terrified him. It is the same kind of reaction I have as I look down from the top of a tremendously tall building or stand at the very rim of the Grand Canyon.

Strangely enough, Moorhouse had no qualifications for attempting this trip. His knowledge of camels came from visits to the London Zoo! He learned Arabic in a crash course for businessmen and practiced the art of navigation with a sextant on the lonely moors of England.

Before his attempt to cross the Sahara, Moorhouse describes his life as one of failure. His marriage had failed, and he realized that a year before the final breakup it was free of all expressions of anger from either partner. They stayed together, not out of consideration or concern, but out of fear; the fear of being lonely and insecure. He describes it this way, "The most insidious form of fear is the fear of being afraid, for it does not simply arrest the [natural] movement; it does not allow it to begin. Yet, if in the face of fear we can summon up the strength and faith to go forward, I think that far more often than not we find that one of two things happens. Either the encounter with the thing feared demonstrates that it is by no means as laden with terrible properties as we had supposed from a distance, a discovery which tends to dissolve the fear itself. Or else, terrible as the encounter may prove to be, it is one which can be endured and which can fortify us in the endurance."[3]

Geoffrey Moorhouse would have found an ally in Fritz Perls, whose belief that anxiety is the stopping block to life is basic to gestalt therapy. He claims that most psychiatrists are afraid of anxiety because they don't know what it is. Our insecurity about the role we have to play produces stagnation and stage fright. Perls wrote, "So the formula of anxiety is very simple: Anxiety is the gap between the *now* and the *then*. If you are in the now, you can't be anxious, because the excitement flows immediately into ongoing spontaneous activity. If you are in the now, you are creative, you are inventive. If you have your senses ready, if you have your eyes and ears open, like every small child, you find a solution."[4]

Perls believed that if there is something you fear, you should launch out and do it. If your reaction to the Sahara is fear, then you have to cross it. Our catastrophic expectations that we cannot survive outside the narrow limits of familiar lifestyles and ingrained self-images can result in neurotic paralysis. To give in to fear, Perls says, "is to remain stuck in the void. When we accept what we fear and go into it, the desert starts to bloom. The empty void becomes the fertile void."[5]

Avoiding Pain

During a conversation, Dr. T. Glynn Williams made an arresting comment to me about fear and human relations: "People need people. The two basic emotions in life are love and fear. People need people, but people are hurt by people and therefore avoid them."

Probably the ultimate Sahara Desert experience for each of us is in this area of human relationships. But we must launch out into relationships—become involved, allow ourselves to get close to people in a venturesome, risky way even though we may be hurt. Williams compares our situation to that of two porcupines on a cold night. They never get closer than they have to for fear of being hurt, but they stay close enough to keep warm and survive.

Why is it so important to conquer our fear and to risk getting hurt—to embark on our own Sahara? For me, Fritz Perls and the gestalt concept provides a significant answer: "All growth stops with the avoidance of pain." When something very traumatic has happened to you; when something painful has been denied, repressed, and buried in some way, all growth stops. But when it is confronted, pain is usually bearable. It is the fear of the pain that causes emotional and physical havoc.

One principle clearly ascribed to at the Menninger Foundation is that often our attempts to avoid pain can destroy us. To avoid dealing with our fears, we drink, overwork, take pills, engage in illicit sex, attempt suicide, and suffer psychosomatic illnesses of all kinds. We cannot bear to be depressed, fearful, or anxious, so we embrace all kinds of life-destroying behavior.

To face suffering, real or imagined, present or future, is to grow. R. D. Laing believes that society today is stunted because we hide or put away all visible signs of suffering. The experiences of birth, death, and mental breakdown are generally hidden behind the walls of institutions so the rest of us need not see them. Laing feels that our own lives will be enriched and our capacity for growth enhanced if on a day-to-day basis we are intimately involved with those who are giving birth, who are suffering, who are having emotional breakdowns, who are dying. But by its very actions society seems to say, "Put these people somewhere out of sight and let the specialists deal with them."

One of the founding staff members of Burrswood Hospital is Marina Chavchavadze, a former Russian princess. Marina's family fled the revolution and arrived penniless in England. Her greatest fear, she told me, was that she would never again have the means to live graciously and comfortably. Very early in her life as a refugee, she vowed, "I'll never marry a poor man. I refuse to darn socks and clean rooms and do domestic chores. Well, what do you think the Lord did? He brought me here to Burrswood to clean floors and scrub and cook for twenty-five years. He knew my fear was hindering me, and I couldn't argue with him. I ended up by enjoying it, you see. And once I began to enjoy it, I was released. As long as I feared this kind of a life, I had to do it."

The Need for Action

Keith Miller gave me some helpful insight on dealing with particular fears or anxiety-producing situations. He says first of all that people need to think through their options in a situation: "Here is a guy who is stuck somehow. He doesn't know what to do vocationally and he's upset about his wife. I might say to him, either about a marriage problem or about a job situation, 'What do you think your options are? What are the first things that you could do?' This is after a lot of discussion, of course." Then Keith suggests a wide variety of options, even bizarre ones like shooting the boss or running off to Mexico with the company funds. In their discussion they try to list ten options without giving any thought as to whether they are impractical or unsuitable. Rather, the important thing is to get the person's "possibility thinking" started so he can brainstorm all sorts of options and check out any real possibilities.

In our discussion Keith mentioned one man who had worried for years over a job change. He had agonized as to whether or not he should leave his secular job and become a minister. When they got down to checking real possibilities, the man called the only seminary he wanted to attend and discovered that they wouldn't accept him because of his poor college record. What a relief! Now he could cross off that option and go back to his job with the assurance that the ministry was not a viable possibility for him.

To summarize Keith's thinking: analyze the fear, consider

carefully all the options, and then move out and act boldly.

This idea is validated by Dr. Robert Soskin. "I think at some point you have to say to the fearful person, 'Look. You can analyze these fears and analyze them and analyze them. But until you go into the fear situation, work with it and deal with it, there ain't nothing going to happen. You can stand outside of what you fear indefinitely. But you have within yourself the resources and the strengths to face and confront that fear situation, and you've got to do it.' "

The Ultimate Risk

Finally, there is no way to deal with fear and risk without facing the fear of death and the risk of our very existence. Theologian Paul Tillich called death the fear of non-being. Death symbolizes the end of life as we know it and the end of relationships as we know them. It is a state in which I am no longer able to redeem any of my unfulfilled relationships. The fear of death is so widespread and universal that perhaps by confronting this specific fear we can find clues about dealing with all of our fears.

We have the same difficulty facing the reality of death that our Victorian ancestors had facing the fact of sex. Sex was that unclean thing hidden away and made the subject of dirty jokes. Geoffrey Gorer, the anthropologist, maintains that ordinary men and women know very well what death is all about since it is also what life is all about. But contemporary theologians—except for fundamentalists—answer questions about death either with amusement or silence or by pretending not to understand the question.[6]

I have certainly come to believe that death and life are intertwined irrevocably. To understand death is to understand life. To accept death is to accept life. To live life to the full, with all its risks, is in some way to accept death. A person living fully now has less fear about death than someone living provisionally—one who is holding back, waiting for some future time to live, relate, accomplish, or risk.

Laing expressed his feelings this way when he spoke to a small group in London in October 1973: "I think it's amazing that we are trying to tuck away the two gates of life, birth and death, as obscene. I hope that when I die I won't be sort of put three-quarters of the way into the morgue. I hope to die within the fabric of my life. I mean, if I'm dying, I wouldn't like my children to be taken out of the room. . . . I'd like them to be part of it, to see it, and to be with it."

It seems to me that the task of the church is to prepare people to die as well as to live. But since this task has not been assumed by the Christian church in any significant way in our time, we find instead a number of secular groups preparing people to face death.

Surprisingly enough, at almost every one of the educational workshops I've attended in recent years, there is invariably a course introducing teachers to death education. These secular teachers would like to see death education taught in the public schools at very early ages. It is their feeling that most children encounter death in a relative, a loved one, a neighbor, a friend at an early age and need to be prepared for this.

Perhaps all of us would benefit from such a course. Certainly Elizabeth Kübler-Ross, author of *On Death and Dying*, gives us a great deal of help in this area by describing the five stages that are a part of the dying process, as she has witnessed it.[7] First the person who is dying experiences denial and isolation, the feelings of being all alone and of refusing to believe what is happening. Next there is anger—the "Why me? I've been such a good person" attitude. The third stage she calls bargaining, making promises in return for healing—"I'll go to church every Sunday. . . . I'll help the poor!" In the next stage the patient feels depressed, and in the fifth and final stage he eventually accepts the experience and is reconciled to his death. She suggests that these five stages are not unique to death and dying but apply to many other experiences of loss, such as divorce or crippling illness or the death of a family member.

Nevertheless, in one sense all of the death education in the world does not really enable us to make peace with dying. I think there is something in each of us that makes us believe we will never die, even though we know better. Sigmund Freud believed that in the unconscious every one of us is convinced of his own immortality. In a lecture in April 1974, I heard Dr. Kübler-Ross say that every scrape with death allows us to continue to believe in our own immortality. Perhaps this explains why so many older people I have encountered in the church are focused on the certainty that these are the last days and that the Second Coming of Christ is imminent. To point out that the Apostle Paul had the same certainty and was wrong by at least two thousand years doesn't shake their conviction one bit. Most people believe intuitively that if their life is almost over, then all of life must be waning. If I am near death, then what hope is there that anything good will continue? When I go, God will be closing the curtains on the world. I like to think that my future and the world's future are synonymous.

Perhaps the fear and pain of death can only be overcome as we are able to see it in terms of a prelude to rebirth. From this Christian perspective, we can come to the point of being able to face death realistically. Unless this happens, the fear of death will stop life before the fact of death catches up with us.

To trust in God's promise of a life beyond is the ultimate risk. But the ability to risk at every level is an indication that we are on the way to wholeness. "He who would lose his life . . . shall find it."

Chapter 8

How to Make Your Dreams Come True

How Things Work in Your Home (*And What to Do When They Don't*) is a book I have recently added to my library. I bought it because this is a part of my life in which I have experienced repeated frustrations. When our children were small, I spent many Christmas Eves trying to put together supposedly easy-to-assemble toys. Even when I understood the directions, I never seemed to have the right tools. And all through our married life I have felt intimidated when my wife has asked me to repair simple things around the house. I never knew where to begin or even what equipment to purchase to do the job. But that new book offers the promise that I will never again be humiliated or embarrassed by my inability to fix something around the house.

On a much larger scale, the inability to make our dreams come true—to implement our ideas and make them work—is a source of defeat and frustration for many of us. For instance, though deeply in love with our mate, we may be unable to live creatively and romantically in a marriage. Instead, everything we say and do seems to increase the alienation and misunderstanding. In the same way, parents and children who genuinely love each other may never know how to implement that love in terms of a meaningful, mutually fulfilling, and satisfying relationship.

In any specialized field, it is possible to be a creative person, full of innovative ideas but lacking in the ability to implement them. Unless there is a strategy for selling the ideas, they may never get into use and practice. Even people in positions of leadership—committee chairmen or company presidents—who have valid goals can be thwarted unless they have a strategy for making things happen.

The ability to implement our goals is an important part of wholeness and completeness. The inability to carry out our ideas and feelings in a way that either maximizes relationships or makes a contribution to society as a whole can result in overwhelming frustration. This may lead to emotional and physical breakdown and ultimately be detrimental to the society itself.

Many couples who marry and have a family can attest to the truth of what we have just said. They find that, "for some reason, things are not working out as we had planned." Their dream is to establish a home where both parents and children may grow and mature in a happy, loving climate. This dream is often backed up by costly and strenuous sacrifice—meals faithfully prepared, laundry done regularly, moonlighting and extra jobs taken on to provide "the things my parents couldn't afford to give me." The dream is there, the price is paid daily; yet the result is often disharmony, alienation, hatred, and sometimes even personality disorders.

Anthropologist Jules Henry has written a poignant and brilliant book entitled *Pathways to Madness*[1] in which he tells the story of five American families, each of which had produced one disturbed institutionalized child. The book deals less with the sources of insanity than with the strange and complex relationships that take place in all too many families.

Henry or his assistant lived for a time with each family, following their patterns, rhythms, schedules; remaining at home with mothers and children during the day; observing the father's homecoming; and then spending evenings with the entire family. The book is a moving description of people who mean well and who are destroying one another. Henry remarks that all of these people are very much like most of us even though each family emerges as a unique entity.

The book describes one family that is bent on making artificial happiness a way of life. They live a lie and are committed to making sure that lie endures. The parents married each other because they felt they couldn't do any better on the marriage market. But they refuse to admit to themselves, their three sons, or others how dissatisfied they are. They insist that their sons believe their lie and that they see their parents as loving and happy and themselves as loved and happy. But two of the sons see through this phony front and are driven to despair as they feel the sham and lovelessness around them. Only the youngest son, a twelve-year-old, learns to believe the lie. He becomes a mirror image for the parents of their illusions about themselves. The parents become paranoid about the two older boys and insist they are trying to destroy them, with the result that one of the older brothers breaks down mentally and must be hospitalized. To the parents, the older sons are seen as problems and the youngest as an angel.

Where to Begin

How can a person learn to implement those personal goals and desires to which he is most committed and about which he feels most strongly? Let me begin with an approach which is being used effectively in any number of therapeutic disciplines. It is based on the conviction that we cannot begin to implement present goals creatively while blaming others for our problems. Dr. Robert Soskin worked for a time with inmates in a large prison. He discovered that something positive happens to the prisoner if he becomes able to say, "Now that I'm here what can I learn from this? How can I grow? How can being here help me become what I want in one, five, or ten years?" When he stops blaming other people for his circumstances, he begins to grow and his entire outlook on life becomes positive and creative.

Perhaps the next step in learning to implement our goals is being able to accept the fact that occasionally we will hurt other people. Dr. T. Glynn Williams of the Maryland Psychiatric Research Center, made this comment in a personal conversation: "You cannot live in a world without doing violence to it. We live off of plants and animals and destroy them to live. In the same way we live off of people and people live off of us, and if we can't handle that, we break down." It is possible that some necessary action on my part might possibly injure or deprive another. If I cannot accept that, I am paralyzed by inaction. Only in a comatose state can we avoid the risk of doing damage to others, but even then we would be a financial and physical burden on those around us. In one sense we do live off of one another, and even our efforts to help another may prove more harmful than helpful. This kind of risk is common in surgery or psychotherapy, and even parents can inflict hurt and harm in their efforts to love and care for their children.

To get involved deeply with another person is risky, and the results may not always prove beneficial. And so often pain and suffering are inflicted by those who presumably are acting in our best interests. We certainly don't want to be hurt, and we don't want to hurt others. But it is essential to our growth that as we move through life we stop blaming others for what happens to us and we stop feeling guilty about any pain we may inadvertently have caused.

Effectiveness through Selectivity

We cannot begin to implement our goals creatively until we have been able to isolate them very clearly. What precisely are the dreams we alone have the vision and motivation to make come true? We cannot do all things in all circumstances at all times. Viktor Frankl said in a talk in San Francisco, "Unless man wishes to drown . . . he has to become selective. That is to say, he has to become able to select when to turn on the TV set, when to turn it off, what books and what journals to read and what to throw in the wastebasket. Selectiveness means that we have to be responsible for what is important and what is not, what is essential and what is not, what is valuable and what is not, what is meaningful and what is not. We have to be capable or become capable of such decision-making."[2]

Now unless I am capable of such decision-making, I can be made to feel guilty by parents, teachers, newspapers, or even my TV set—indeed by everything around me—about the things I am not learning, reading, being, or doing. My conscience must decide those things that are meaningful for me and those things that are necessary to implement the unique personal goals that are mine alone. This requires some maturity and a certain amount of planned neglect. It may mean suffering the slings and arrows of people around us who are clamoring insistently for us to do their thing or help them with their thing. This kind of selectivity may even look like selfishness. But, on the other hand, life can be wasted in riotous nonselectivity.

William Shutz, in a University of Maryland workshop in 1974, spoke of selectivity in relationships. "With regard to strangers, people who don't mean much to me, (the waitress, cashiers, and people I meet peripherally) it is a matter of conscious choice in terms of my own values. That is, if I'm going out of the restaurant and I don't like what the cashier did to me just now I can either spend the next half hour encountering her or I can get on with what I wanted to do.

And usually I'll choose to get on with what I wanted to do because that's more important to me than being pure in the sense of being totally honest at all points with all people."

Shutz is warning us that to be pure in every relationship would consume all of one's time. It is impossible to encounter every person we meet with total love or honesty and still fulfill our selective goals. In some relationships we must often settle for more superficial levels of contact. There are times when we must ignore unfulfilling relationships and focus instead on those relationships that are essential to the accomplishment of our goals and purposes.

Handling Opposition

Another block in implementing our personal goals can be our insensitivity to the realities of the present situation. Kurt Lewin has called this the force-field analysis. In any situation where certain forces are pushing for change, there are always other forces holding back or restraining change. It is the balance between those two forces that keep the situation the way it is, according to Lewin, and before we implement a change, we ought to get in contact with those forces. The prime question in implementing change is, "What do you have going for you and what do you have against you?"

Suppose, for example, you are a teacher trying to innovate change in your school system. In your attempt you have alienated the principal; your program sounds scary to the P.T.A., the school board thinks it will be expensive; and the other teachers feel threatened by it. On the plus side, perhaps you have a handful of enthusiastic students and one or two friends in the system who are in favor of your innovations. You will have to learn to sell yourself and your idea to those on the negative side before the process of change can become a reality.

What approach can we use with people who are negative about our ideas for change? I am reminded of the two priests in training who wanted to change some of the monastery rules. They both smoked and were suffering because they were not allowed to smoke during prayers. Each young priest decided to talk to his superior about the problem. One came back from his interview dejected. "No luck," he said, "I asked if I could smoke while I prayed and the answer was 'No!' " "Well, I don't think you asked the right question," replied the other. "I said, 'Father, I have a terrible addiction to smoking. Is it all right for me to pray while I'm smoking?' His answer was, 'Bless you, my son. You can pray anytime.' " The phrasing of the question may have a determining effect on the answer.

Relational Sensitivity

But however much we are able to understand and clarify our goals and assess our talents for implementing those goals, we are eventually faced with the fact that implementation is not possible without other people. We must have some skill in relationships if our ideas are to be transmitted to other people.

This truth is perhaps most apparent in the classroom. Think of the teachers who have a genuine dream for helping young people maximize their skills and talents for life. Some of these teachers have turned down higher paying jobs in industry because of their commitment. But often a mistaken strategy can produce results quite different from the original dream. Perhaps the dream goes awry most often because they think they are teaching subject matter instead of people.

Jules Henry, in the book mentioned earlier, comments on what often happens in classrooms. He describes a boy who stands helplessly at the blackboard unable to solve an equation. From the rows of waving hands the teacher finally selects a girl who delights in giving the right answer. This is no mere lesson in mathematics, Henry claims. This is a demonstration of the geometry of humiliation. What is actually taught is the fact that the success of one person can be achieved at the expense of another. What we learn is to hate others who are successful and we become determined to prevent anyone from succeeding at our expense.

Dr. Thomas Gordon, Director and founder of Parent Effectiveness Training, is trying to help parents improve their relational skills as a means of implementing their dreams for their children. He made these significant comments at the White House Conference on Children: "We need to find an effective way to modify those human relationships that exert the most influence on children's psychological health. Namely, the parent/child relationship and the teacher/student relationship. Modifying these relationships is a critical requirement for preventing psychological disorders in the society. . . . Despite the fact that most parents sincerely want to raise emotionally healthy children, we have ample evidence that far too few parents possess the skills to do it. One of the reasons for parents' ineffectiveness, of course, is that few ever received training for the job of parenthood. In fact, most parents in our society still believe that they can enter into parenthood inherently equipped to do an effective job. It is not a commonly held belief in our society that being an effective parent might require special training, just as surely as being effective in any other endeavor."[3]

Students of Parent Effectiveness Training are helped to meet their own needs and actualize their effectiveness within a relationship, while helping the other person to do the same. They commit themselves to a no-lose method of resolving conflict by finding a solution acceptable to both parties.

Some questions have been raised about this approach for reasons that were expressed bluntly by R. D. Laing during an interview. "God help us if we start having training in being human." Laing fears we will soon proceed from training in personal sensitivity to holding competition to see who is the most sensitive or the most human. It is clear that he feels one can be just as plastic in relationships with this new method as one was in the old patterns. Perhaps there is no safe program in implementing our relational abilities. Like some surgery, the program may prove fatal but we are dying without it.

Implementation through Communication

Basic to all good and healthy relationships is the ability to communicate—to communicate feelings and ideas so that they are understood. Communication is essential to the implementation of ideas in society, business, the church, the world.

One of our problems in communication, however, is that no two people ever hear the same thing. This is one of the pitfalls of mass education. If you pass out a book to thirty students and ask them to read the material and report on it, you have already created an unfair premise because each of the students has a unique set of experiences, emotions, feelings, apprehensions, and dreams that he brings to the material. There is no such thing as an objective communication, only subjective communication.

In addition, though—and this is rather tricky—people often have a need to believe they have heard something which they haven't. For example, three California medical educators, Naftulin, Ware, and Donnelly, devised a hoax for experimental purposes. They hired a professional actor, gave him fictitious credentials, and had him lecture on "Mathematical Game Theory As Applied to Physical Education" to a group of psychiatrists, psychologists, and educators. Billed as "Dr. Myron L. Fox of the Albert Einstein University," the actor lectured, employing academic jargon and double-talk, citing one irrelevant, conflicting, and meaningless statement after another. His question and answer period was even more irrelevant and meaningless. When his lecture was finished, a questionnaire was distributed to the audience on which they would respond anonymously to Dr. Fox's talk. There were extravagant comments such as, "Excellent presentation." "Enjoyed listening." "He had a warm manner." "Good flow."

"Seems enthusiastic." "Lively examples." "Extremely articulate." "Too intellectual." Not one of the educators realized their authoritative lecturer was a phony. All were convinced they had learned something.[4]

Another difficulty in communication is that the facts we are given depend somewhat on the nature of our relationship with the teller. So the "truth" I am told is not the "truth" you are told about the same situation. Efforts are made in an attempt to offset this problem at Burrswood Hospital in England. At staff meetings the orderlies, nurses, doctors, and specialists all come together and report on their conversations with the same patient. By piecing together what people tell about themselves to a number of different people in different roles, they get a more realistic picture of what's really happening to the patient, at least as he or she understands it.

Transactional analysis has given us many helpful guidelines in good communication but particularly by pointing out that there are three people in each of us, the parent, adult and child. Good communication takes place, Eric Berne says, when my parent talks to your parent, my child to your child or my adult to your adult. Bad communication starts with cross transactions, when your parent talks to my child or my adult to your parent. Berne's classic illustration of this is in a transaction between a husband and wife where the husband asks, "Dear, where are my cufflinks?" (an adult, seeking information.) A complimentary response by wife would be, "In your top left dresser drawer." If she bellows, "Where you left them!" the result is a cross transaction. The stimulus was adult but the wife turned the response over to the parent.

A *Strategy for Groups*

Finally, how can I implement my ideas, as well as those from other people, in an organization or group in order to make my dreams come true? Organizations are organic and don't respond to rigid rules any better than individuals do. Someone has said that to understand how organizations work you have to pay more attention to the alleys than to the highways. The constitution and the by-laws are less important to the machinery of an organization than the alleyways of personal relationships and interrelationships that take place. Beyond the rules, one must know something about the history and the dynamics of the relationships among the people of any given organization.

On one occasion Robert McNamara was asked by a friend of mine what single problem he considered most serious among all those he inherited when he became head of the Ford Motor Company. "My biggest problem," responded McNamara, "is that nobody wants to tell me what is going on. Everybody tells me what they want me to hear or what they think I want to hear." In any organization or group setting, we had better recognize that the success of the organization is secondary to the ego, future, and security of the individuals and departments concerned. Truth becomes an elusive thing—not intentionally, but by default.

We frequently experience frustration because we are unable to bring our dreams to fruition through the organizations and groups of which we are a part. But it is only as we take into account the personal needs of the people in the organization that we can begin to understand and explore the alleyways that block the path to new goals.

Two very helpful insights have come to my attention which offer an approach for implementing ideas in any group or organization. One is the concept of leadership or management by objective. This simply means that we no longer function on the basis of solving problems—the technique used by most businesses, churches, and families. Rather, management by objective means deciding on valid, satisfying goals for a particular group and then carefully determining the precise steps essential to achieving them. Of primary importance also is the provision for regular time to evaluate progress.

The second insight is in the area of leadership style. After a group or organization has decided on objectives and is launched on a course, good leadership is crucial. Leadership can cripple or impede, or it can be the creative force that makes progress possible. Ted Engstrom and Edward Dayton, effective seminar leaders and writers on the subject of management, have come up with some helpful classifications of leadership style. It seems to me these leadership styles are applicable quite apart from our participation in any complex organizational structure. Most of us fit into one of these categories whether we are chairing a church or civic commitee or supervising a part-time cleaning woman.

There is the *bureaucratic leader,* whose style is marked by continual reference to rules and regulations; the *permissive leader,* whose desire is to keep everyone in the group satisfied —keeping people happy is the name of the game; the *laissez-faire* leader, who gives practically no leadership at all—everything is left to run on its own course; the *participative leader* —who believes the way to motivate others is to involve them in the decision-making process; the *autocratic leader,* who relies on authority and usually assumes people will not do anything unless told.[5]

Instinctively each of us is one type or another. And hopefully there is a place for all types at different times in most groups and organizational settings. It is important that a leader develop styles other than the one which comes naturally. It takes a combination of styles to be effective over the long haul.

Buried in the Christian church is a concept that could possibly revolutionize the lives of all of its members. It is the concept of the priesthood of believers. It is my understanding that this simply means that I am not only accountable to God and responsible for my own behavior, I am also, under God, accountable to my brothers and sisters and in a sense responsible for their behavior. What would happen if we took advantage of that kind of help from one another? Others could help me set uniquely authentic goals, monitor my performance, ride herd on my self-defeating behavior and attitude, and help me discover hidden talents, gifts, and resources for the accomplishment of those goals. If wholeness is to come to any of us, I don't believe it will come in splendid isolation. But as a part of the body of Christ, loving one another, we are responsible for helping each other dream—the largest dreams possible. Beyond that we must help each other find ways to make those dreams come true.

Chapter 9

Cultivate the Ah-Ha Moments

During the first semester our daughter was in law school, she was absolutely terrified, not so much by the amount of work, which was staggering, but by the fact that for the first time in her life what she was learning didn't always seem to make sense. But somehow that magical moment came when she began to see the interrelatedness of all the phases of law that she had been studying. In that moment of "ah-ha," she began to understand where it all fit together. Her studies are still a struggle, but now she is able to handle them creatively.

Medical students have told me much the same story. At first it is overwhelming, but then the day comes when all the anatomy and chemistry of the body with its thousands of identifiable parts comes together into a whole. This can happen to all of us in more commonplace ways. If you are trying to learn to play the piano, it seems impossible at first to integrate the reading of music on the printed page with timing and finger dexterity. But then one day everything falls into place and you find yourself playing not just the notes but real music.

The Action-Producing Concepts

To each of us have come these decisive and pivotal moments of insight or wisdom or illumination. It was as if we were in a darkened room, but then the drapes were pulled open by an unseen hand and the room was flooded with brilliant light. The pieces of the puzzle were seen with new perspective and in a new relationship.

To some extent, our level of expectancy is one factor that determines whether or not certain things come together for us. "As a man thinketh, so is he," says the Bible. And it does seem that the perpetual pessimist is inevitably the victim of unhappy circumstances, while the born optimist leads a kind of charmed life, sailing through obstacles with uncanny ability. But this is not surprising. It is really a short step from belief to habits, for habits are after all an application of beliefs. Without something constructive to live for, how does one remain healthy?

Robert A. Clark, an associate professor of clinical psychiatry, wrote this about the healthy balance he saw in Carl Jung's life. "Jung was a fascinating combination of extroversion and introversion. He enjoyed people of all sorts and was interested in each one. At the same time he had an active and profound inner life. He was able to bury himself for months at a time in his country house in Bollingen to read, meditate, paint and write."[8]

We cannot live all of life in the ah-ha or insight-filled dimension. Much of life requires action. The notion shared by some young people today that life can be spent in meditation and contemplation without action is utterly false and unworkable.

Pivotal Moments

I still relive those moments of illumination when some creative concept changed my philosophy and ministry and personal approach to life. For example, I will never forget sitting in my room at seminary with my head whirling with doubts about God. It was Saturday afternoon and all of my friends and classmates were off on assignments. I was alone in my despair. The bright light which seemed to lead me into the ministry had gone off. As I came upon the book *Mere Christianity* by C. S. Lewis[2] and began to read, suddenly doubt became something understandable and manageable and the very substance on which faith was built. In those electric moments my faith was reborn and I felt able to continue.

A few years later, C. S. Lewis gave me another one of those moments while I was flying to the funeral of a young friend. Quite overwhelmed with grief and questions, I began to read *The Great Divorce*.[3] His description of the geography, landscape, and strategy of heaven and hell spoke to me. I realized hell is a place that people choose, not a place to which they are sent. And heaven is a place people choose and are willing to enter on God's terms. Ever since that day, I have lived in the shadow of the glory and wonder of God's grace as revealed in a future with a possible heaven and a possible hell.

Another "ah-ha" moment came to me through Paul Tournier. I had taken clinical training after seminary to learn more about the art of counseling. Everything that I had learned up to that time emphasized the idea that a counselor does not identify with nor become involved with his counselees. But it had been my experience that when I was a real person with struggling people, God seemed to bring help or healing. When I tried to be professional and neutral and nondirective, I did not see any results. In *The Meaning of Persons*, Tournier suggests that the counselor's own humanity is his greatest resource in helping another. When the counselor lowers his mask, the counselee can lower his, and in the dialogue between real people growth and healing may take place.[4] That moment of insight and understanding which Tournier has brought to so many of us validated my own experience.

In my first pastorate I read Elton Trueblood's *Your Other Vocation*, and I discovered through the eyes and the heart of this gifted man that God's strategy for accomplishing his will in the world is primarily through lay people and that we clergy are to be servants of the laity. The lay person is more than an usher or church officer or someone who might paint the church basement on a free Saturday. The laity are called to a ministry of liberation.[5]

Sam Shoemaker gave me a similar creative concept in his insistence on nonpious conversion. Previously, I had considered conversion the sole domain of the superpious, the fundamentalist, the spiritual, or the Pentecostal. Shoemaker talked about conversion as God's gift to every believer irrespective of his particular theological position. Conversion was the point at which God changed a person's life, and this experience did not require either pious language or a pious setting.

Another significant moment occurred during a conversation in a skyscraper office in New York. Dr. Howard Keeley, who was then director of the Evangelistic Association of New England, was talking with me about the church. For the first time, I heard someone say that the Bible seems to indicate that the test of orthodoxy is not doctrine but the quality of relationships. For me, the whole concept of relational theology was born at that time—a concept which has been my focus ever since.

Moments of psychological truths as well have shaped my life and thoughts and ministry. Transactional analysis, for example, with its parent/adult/child theory, has helped me and countless others to see the three changing roles in which we live—why we turn some people on and others off. This insight helps us to communicate as real people without falling into the old patterns of dialogue which have proven so frustrating and which cause such a stalemate in relationships.

Another life-changing insight came to me from Carl Jung in just one simple paragraph. He pointed out that self-hate was the very heart of sin. I had always known that to hate anyone, including, or especially, your enemies, was not Christian. But to hate one's self had always seemed respectable, humble, and even desirable. Jung's one paragraph about the difficulty of loving one's self opened a new relationship with myself in the light of God's grace.

These and other creative concepts have been milestones for me in discovering truth—how to live it and how to communicate it. But we should not limit these creative concepts simply to the intellectual dimension. Insight can come in every area of life, which will change not just our behavior but our very life on this planet.

Intuition and Intellect

I think it's important at this point to understand that, in referring to creative concepts, I am not solely concerned with intellectual concepts. Harvard biologist and historian Everett I. Mendelson reflects the growing disillusionment with the intellectual and academic dimensions of life that many Americans have been undergoing in recent years. He says, "Science as we know it has outlived its usefulness."

Psychologist Fritz Perls puts it this way, "Intuition is the intelligence of the organism. Intelligence is the whole, and intellect is the whore of intelligence—the computer . . . all this figuring out by which many people replace *seeing and hearing what's going on.* Because if you are busy with your computer, your energy goes into your thinking, and you don't see and hear anymore."[6] And Albert Wiggam has said that intelligence seems to be the thing that enables people to get along without education. Education appears to enable a person to get along without the use of intelligence.

The new age we're entering, I believe, will be marked by an awareness of the creative concept—the intuitive rather than intellectual approach. Beyond the rational or intellectual is the truth in our hearts and minds and, indeed, in the heart of the universe itself. Abraham Maslow said, "We have learned to think of knowledge as verbal, explicit, articulated, rational, logical, aristotelian, realistic, sensible. Equally important are mystery, ambiguity, illogical contradiction, and transcendent experience."[7]

Hopefully, it is not a case of either/or. There is a place for the scientific and the rational, but we have overplayed them and have minimized the mystical and the intuitive. Richard H. Bube, Professor of Electrical Engineering at Stanford University, has said, "One of the most pernicious falsehoods ever to be almost universally accepted is that the scientific method is the only reliable way to truth."[8]

Encouraging the Ah-Ha Moments

It's obvious by now, I'm sure, that we're trying here to come to grips with something beyond expanded consciousness and broader than intellectualization. We're grappling with the fact of wisdom itself; what it is, how it comes to us, and how it can change life for us and for those around us. How can a person who has never experienced the ah-ha moment of brilliant beautiful truth find it? Or how can a person who has once lived in that dimension rediscover it? For the Christian, this may be the still small voice within, through which we believe God is speaking. Many people discipline themselves and practice a quiet time—a set time when they listen for God's voice and the ideas that come from him. I find this very helpful. Frequently the thoughts and ideas that come from these times of disciplined quiet and listening take the form of specific guidance.

Some historians have said that Thomas Edison "invented the twentieth century," a claim difficult to dispute. We live near his winter home in Fort Myers, Florida, and hundreds of stories are circulated in this area about his eccentric genius. My favorite concerns his daily fishing routine. Every day after lunch, he spent several hours alone fishing on a 300-foot pier that had been constructed on his riverfront property. But here is the catch—he never used bait or hooks for fear that catching fish would interrupt his thoughts.

I think Edison would have understood and appreciated all of our contemporary attempts to cultivate the ah-ha moments of our lives. My friend and editor, Floyd Thatcher, wrote me recently about his own experience of cultivating such moments. "In my case, when I am consciously searching for a solution or a creative idea—after I've worked on it consciously—I deliberately put it out of my mind and mow the lawn or play golf. It is in those moments when my mind is at rest in a completely changed environment that the ideas come. I think this can be conscious discipline. Also, when I am at my best, I utilize the power of affirmation, sometimes from 'deep relaxation.' Other times just through the repetitive process right in the midst of the rush of life. I find, again when I am at my best, that a powerful affirmation for me is 'I can do all things through Christ who strengthens me.' And I believe 'all things' includes a sharpening of the creative process—the flow of ideas. For me this is God at work in the deepest and most complex areas of our lives—areas which we Christians have tended to ignore because of our emphasis on the cognitive aspects of our faith. Really now—so much of our pious emphasis on faith tends to be phony; we want to *know*—we want to know on a cognitive level and our insistence on that dulls our ability to hear the still, small voice."

You may identify more with Floyd Thatcher than Thomas Edison, but it's probably futile to copy either of them. Each of us is unique, and there is a place and time that is best for us. It has taken me half a lifetime to learn that. For years, I tried to copy the devotional or meditational habits of some past or present spiritual hero in my life, usually with disappointing results. But if you believe in a God who wants to illuminate your mind and guide your path, you'll probably be more receptive at a time or in a place where your guard is down and it is not forced.

For some people, this low-resistance threshold occurs just before they drop off to sleep at night. For others, it is during the first waking moments in the morning. Or you may do your most intense meditating while jogging or listening to music. One friend of mine gets her best thoughts while darning the family's socks.

Quite by accident, I made the embarrassing discovery that my best hunches, ideas, and creativity come during my hot morning shower, not kneeling before the altar on a cold chapel floor between 5:00 and 6:00 A.M. In mental hospitals, hot baths are often used to curb hostile or anxious patients; but in my case, I can testify that hot water applied externally, combined with no inner pressure to seem spiritual or profound, seems to work with some degree of consistency to produce my personal ah-ha moments.

A Flash of Truth

I have described at some length how some of my ah-ha moments have shaped my theology and my ministry. But God has given me pictures of truth, as he does all of us, at a number of points in my life. I have acted on them somewhat impetuously but most of them seem even in retrospect to have been valid.

The first time I dated my wife, I proposed to her. I couldn't explain it, but I knew she was the girl I had been looking for all my life. It just didn't seem necessary to test the relationship over a prolonged period of time.

Now we live on a barrier island in the Gulf of Mexico off the West Coast of Florida. The first time I saw this island I knew I wanted to live here, and we bought a lot. I had looked for this place all my life, and when the reality matched the picture inside me, illogically, maybe, but with great conviction, I believed this was the place God had me for now.

In the same way, I believe that many people, caught up

in great causes, are committed to them because they have had similar flashes of truth. Through a set of circumstances, they realize that this is their *kairos*—the moment of opportunity—and they seize it. They hurl themselves into that cause believing that their presence and their decisive action could be the deciding factor for that spiritual, political, educational, or social struggle at this moment in time.

How else could a man like William Wilberforce, the diminutive hunchback, have been motivated and enabled almost single-handedly to end the slave trade in the British Empire? Perhaps it was that intuitive flash of truth that assured him the right time was at hand. I can't help believing that such an intuitive moment might explain the actions of Rosa Parks in Montgomery, Alabama, who, after years of quietly accepting second-class status, decided one day that she had ridden in the back of the bus long enough.

By sheer necessity most of us will continue to make the majority of our decisions rationally and cognitively. It is true that we cannot live only on the level of creative concepts—the intuitive, the ah-ha moments. But I believe that for many it is in this dimension that God is eager to open up new worlds and reveal his will in a remarkably different way to each of us.

Earlier in this chapter I mentioned Carl Jung, who is one of my heroes. One dimension of his great genius lay in his capacity to cultivate and expect creative concepts. Toward the end of his life he wrote, "I can scarcely keep pace and must watch out that the creative forces do not chase me around the universe at a gallop. . . . I have to coax myself . . . not to do too much." Then, after a serious heart attack in 1946, he wrote, "It seems as if I am ready to die, although some powerful thoughts are still flickering like lightnings in a summer night."[9]

Chapter 10

Understanding Your Body

Obviously it would be both foolish and impossible to define the components of wholeness without including the need for a positive relationship to one's body. I cannot be a whole person if I do not understand my body, accept my body, learn from my body, cooperate with my body and enjoy my body. My body is not a container in which I live. I am my body and my body is me.

We read evidence almost every day of new discoveries about the interrelatedness of body, mind, and spirit from medicine, psychology, and psychiatry. Even in theology, from our Judeo-Christian tradition we are recovering a basic truth long obscured by the Western world's love of Greek philosophy. It is fascinating to note that in Hebrew there is no term to designate the physical body exclusively. In Hebrew, the original language of the Old Testament Scriptures, the word *basar*, usually translated as "flesh" or "body," means the whole person. *Nephesh*, commonly translated as "soul," means the same thing. So the words that have come to us in English as body and soul did not originally have separate meanings. Both words denote the whole person.

The Unity of Body, Mind, and Spirit

But even beyond this linguistic distinction, the very theology of the Bible, both the Old and the New Testament, is basically incarnational. The Bible is not essentially a book about ideas. Rather it is about the birth and life and death of persons, families and nations. Blaise Pascal, on the night of his conversion made this same discovery. He wrote, "God! The God of Abraham, Isaac and Jacob! The God of Jesus Christ! *Not* the God of the philosophers and the scholars!" Pascal felt there was no way to understand biblical history apart from incarnation and the life, death, and continuation of people. The biblical message is not disembodied theological concepts, and it cannot be separated from the bodies of the people in and through whom God lives and moves.[1]

In many ways, the evangelistic efforts of the church today are beginning to embrace this concept. Along with sharing the spiritual good news of Christianity, there is a growing concern for the physical well-being of the hearers. We are beginning to emphasize the kind of total ministry practiced by Jesus himself, who raised the dead, healed the sick, and fed the hungry. In the past we have been guilty of separating the physical and spiritual in our personal ministry to each other as well. But we cannot help people deal with problems of resentment, lack of faith, or the inability to pray and ignore their problems with sleeplessness, overweight, or destructive sex.

Historically, there have always been those religious leaders who equated spirituality with physical denial. Abraham Maslow was speaking to this when he denounced the philosophical fallacy of the mystics and the ascetics. In a San Francisco address he said, "You don't have to mortify the flesh. You can enjoy the flesh ten times more. It's the same continuum. It's just part of the same thing. The spiritual life or the higher life is absolutely not mutually exclusive with bodily life or the fleshly life." Maslow further believes that people who live the more spiritual ascetic life are usually able to live more vigorously in the physical life and to enjoy the body.

Understanding Illness

Dr. Aubert of Burrswood Hospital told the following story about a patient who had been brought to him very reluctantly some five years before. The young woman was a nurse who had given up her profession because she had developed rheumatoid arthritis. She had multiple swollen joints, pyrexia, lassitude, and all the usual symptoms. After two years of being bedridden, she improved enough to train as a teacher, a physically less-exacting profession. She had taught for two years when the arthritis flared up once more and brought her to a standstill. By the time she came to see Dr. Aubert, she had been out of work for three years, and for two of those she had been almost entirely bedridden. He persuaded her to come to Burrswood as an in-patient.

She was an intelligent young woman, on the surface rather a cool customer with little apparent emotion. One day, however, during a misunderstanding, she exploded. It was clear that underneath the cool exterior, fierce fires were burning. Dr. Aubert describes the interview and relationship from there. "Inside we found a number of fierce and bitter resentments. Bitterness because she was an adopted child. Bitterness that she was a homosexual. Bitterness that this had not been understood by those in her church. Bitterness against her mother for being overpossessive. We also noticed that every time she blew her top all her joints became inflamed noticeably. I asked her to consider the possibility that her illness was nothing else than the effect of this tremendous turbulent emotion on her physical body, with the main impact being on her joints. This was something she was prepared to accept. Gradually, as her hostility to the church, to life—and this really meant also to God—began to evaporate her illness began to improve. After a period of about a year, she lost all her symptoms. The pain went, the swelling went, the lassitude went. Her rheumatologist pronounced her perfectly well."

After telling this story, Dr. Aubert added this important word. "By no means does everybody who has rheumatoid arthritis have it because they have these innate, bottled-up, aggressive emotions." But in this instance, at least, the evidence seems clear that by understanding the causes of her illness, this patient was helped to overcome it. Dr. Aubert explains that the goal at Burrswood is the ultimate wholeness of the body, mind, and soul intended by God for man from the beginning. He believes that all genuine modes of healing originate from the divine source of all healing, whether this is mediated through medical or spiritual means.

Reading Your Body

Gestalt therapy encourages all of us to read our own bodies. It believes, with growing evidence and logic, that each person's body is a repository of the spiritual, emotional, and psychic struggles that are taking place. Your body can tell you a great deal about what is happening to the rest of you. If this is possible, then it follows that we could be enabled to read the bodies of others. This kind of gift need not be confined to people with psychic or mystic powers.

There was one such mystic at Esalen while I was there. Body reading was her specialty, and she worked with most of the members of our small gestalt group. She gave a physical reading after an hour's examination of each person's body. The exam entailed checking the seven life centers and discovering blockages. She then interpreted what was going on in your life on the basis of her findings. Our group included all kinds of intellectual types, people one would scarcely consider gullible, who were stunned by the accuracy of her diagnosis.

The Body Is a Friend and Teacher

A person's body is more than a collection of chemicals, tubes, bones, and skin. My body is no more than I am nor any less than I am—it is me, a marvelous creation, a gift, and something to be celebrated.

My body is my friend. It's a computer that helps me understand my psyche and my emotions. But even more important, it is that part of me that often suffers the many unresolved emotional conflicts which could destroy me psychically. The whole idea as I understand it behind psychosomatic medicine is that the body carries emotional burdens that we are not mature enough or secure enough to face. My body is not pain-ridden or obese or unattractive simply to embarrass me. It is carrying a tremendous burden for me.

The body is not only a friend whose existence and presence we can celebrate and enjoy, it is also a teacher. Through the body and its reactions we can learn something of our true feelings. It is quite well established through research studies that we get sick at times of changes in our lives, changes to which we cannot adjust. We tend to fall ill, psychologically or physically or both, when we suffer major losses.

Dr. Walther Lechler, a German psychiatrist, feels that one of the great tragedies in modern medicine is that doctors frequently have the ability and the power to cure people before the true meaning of their illness is discovered. What an amazing idea! In effect he was saying that every illness has some meaning, and we miss the gift that is hidden in our illness if we become well too soon.

I visited Dr. Lechler's clinic in Germany's Black Forest, a facility for one hundred people, each of whom stays an average of three months. Most of the patients who come are taking medicines which, according to Dr. Lechler, only prolong their dull suffering. "They don't feel pain, they just simply don't feel any more. They are paying a high price, a terrible price. They are paying the price of life." Lechler's unusual approach to treating emotional problems comes out of a deep spiritual experience. "With all of my training in medicine and phychiatry, I came to a point of personal dissatisfaction with my own life. When I found the spiritual side of life, I discovered that when you deal with human beings, without relating to God, you're only half a person. You just don't feel at home on this earth. But with the knowledge of a loving Father comes a certainty that you can experience an enjoyable dialogue with life." In that dialogue with life, Walther Lechler believes that our illness has a message for us and we must come to understand the meaning of that message.

Emotions and Illness

There is a great deal of research going on today based on the premise that almost every illness, its recurrence and recovery rate, can be linked to the patient's mind, personality, attitude, and social relationships. One clinician specializing in the treatment of arthritis has documented two hundred and seventy cases in which the patient was cured when he was free from fear, worry, or resentment. This particular doctor believes that at least 60 percent of arthritic cases have their origin in moral conflict.

Similar findings are noted among those studying skin diseases. A team of specialists recently studied the records of more than eleven hundred persons with various skin ailments. In five hundred cases symptoms were linked to emotional causes. Of the cases studied, about 70 percent were suffering from depression, and more than 18 percent were victims of emotional conflicts.

Dr. William Glasser believes that illness itself is, for most of us, a deliberate choice. He seems to feel that many people are sick because they have identified themselves as failures, and he makes this rather startling statement: "If a doctor sees one genuinely sick person in a week in a busy practice, he has a big week. Most of the people he sees have diseases that are products of personal failure."[2]

While Glasser's statements may be hard to prove, there is much to indicate he is largely right. Medicine, psychiatry, education, and religion all seem to be on the threshold of discovering new ways to deal with fears and attitudes and relationships so that the body might be healed. If Glasser is saying, in essence, that we are as sick as we want to be, then there is also ample evidence that we can be as well as we want to be. We read about professional football players who have played an entire game with a broken wrist, nose, toe, or hand. These athletes even claim to have felt no pain at all simply because of the excitement of the contest. We read about aging athletes who continue to excel long beyond the usual retirement age. George Blanda was still playing professional football at forty-five. Sam Snead, in his sixties, gives a good account of himself in golf tournaments.

The fact that the mind and the spirit affect the body seems to have been proven conclusively. Recently a medical research team from the University of North Carolina studied 3,102 residents of Evans County, Georgia, and came up with these conclusions: If you want to avoid a heart attack you should be born black, stay lean, not smoke or engage in excessive physical activity. If you meet those standards, you can eat animal fat, show a high cholesterol level, suffer from cardiac arrhythmia and high blood pressure but still avoid heart disease. Most important, you must never, never rise above the social status of your father. That means trouble for the heart!

Drs. Meyer Friedman and Ray H. Rosenman have done more than fifteen years of study into the causes of heart attack. In their book *Type A Behavior and Your Heart*,[3] these two cardiologists conclude that heart attacks are caused by a person's emotional makeup and not by eating, drinking, or social habits. Their book describes the people who are most apt to suffer heart seizures and calls these people "Type A persons." They make up about half of America's population.

Here are some Type A personality characteristics: "Traits range from explosive accentuation of various key words in ordinary conversation to impatience at the speed things proceed to a vague guilt feeling when they are relaxing willingly or unwillingly."

Another 40 percent of the population is classified as Type B. These people possess all of the drive and intelligence of the Type As but their characteristics steady them, raise their confidence, and increase their sense of security instead of being goads and irritants as they are for the Type A person. Heart disease seldom strikes Type B before seventy, "regardless of the fatty foods eaten, cigarettes smoked, or lack of exercise." Friedman and Rosenman feel that a man's station in life has little or nothing to do with his type. They have found that a sense of job responsibility is not synonymous with the urgency sense of Type A. Presumably Type As are born that way.

Another research study on heart attacks which has been going on at the Menninger Foundation indicates that psychological forces are an important contributing factor in heart attacks. And, "It seems that individuals die when they are no longer able to live because of terminal psychic impairment as well as terminal physical impairment. They feel locked into an intolerable situation from which they see no means of escape. The dilemma has only one road out."[4] They conclude that for some individuals heart attack may represent a socially sanctioned suicide.

As yet no one has linked together the underlying connections among these various studies into the cause of heart attack. But all of the studies, and many more like them, affirm the basic assumption that the body is powerfully affected by the mind, spirit, and attitude of the individual.

The Place of Touch

The concept of the healing touch is enforced throughout the New Testament. We read of Jesus putting mud on the eyes of the blind man to make him see or of a woman healed of an issue of blood by brushing the hem of his garment. The gospel record indicates he laid his hands on many. There is healing in touch. If you won't touch me, I find it hard to believe that you love me. And by the same token, if I am unwilling to be touched, it is difficult for you to love me. I am my body and my body is me. If I need love and relationship and affirmation, then it must come in some way other than through words or attitudes. It must be physically communicated by touch.

Our bodies need to be touched because this is a means of healing our souls and minds. An amazing illustration of the power of touching in healing can be found at the New York University Nursing School, where a course is offered in the laying on of hands. The course is taught by Dr. Delores Krieger, a nurse and associate professor of education who has been practicing the laying on of hands for about two years with great success. She says, "There is no limit to what it can cure—arthritis, fever, backache, anything you care to name. It's something that can produce results when all else fails.

"I tell my students to use their hands like divining rods and try to feel some sort of sensation. Some people feel pricking sensations when they pass their hands over an area of the patient's body where a problem lies. As for myself, I feel extreme heat in my palm. . . . Sometimes I also feel something like a magnetic pull. Once I find the area where the trouble lies, I lay my hands on the patient for between five and twenty minutes. I think consciously all the time about transferring energy from my body to the patient's.

"There is a force that is called prana—which we call vigor—within all of us. Healthy people have more prana than they need, while ill people don't have enough. I discovered prana can be transmitted from one person to another by touch and the desire to heal—and that anyone can do it."

Meaningful Love

Dr. Karl Menninger has said that "love is the medicine for the sickness of the world." If people are literally ill and dying from lack of love, then we must understand that the body is one of our primary means of transmitting that love to one another. Isn't that the message of the incarnation? The first verse of the First Letter of John speaks of "that which was from the beginning, which we have heard, which we have seen with our eyes, which we have looked upon and touched with our hands" (RSV). God's love took a tangible, physical form in Jesus Christ, who lived among us touching and being touched. Ultimately the sacrifice of that physical body became the means of God's great act of loving and healing his world.

Our willingness to touch and be touched is an important dimension of our ability to love. I am indebted to an old friend, Donna Swanson, for her sensitive poem "Minnie Remembers."

> God,
> My hands are old,
> I've never said that out loud before.
> But they are.
> I was so proud of them once.
> They were soft.
> Like velvet smoothness of a firm ripe peach.
> Now the softness is like worn-out sheets
> Or withered leaves.
> When did these slender, graceful hands
> Become gnarled, shrunken?
> They lie here in my lap;
> Naked reminders of the rest of this old body
> That has served me too well.
>
> How long has it been since someone touched me?
> Twenty years?
> Twenty years I've been a widow.
> Respected.
> Smiled at.
> But never touched.
> Never held close to another body.
> Never held so close and warm that loneliness was
> Blotted out.

I remember how my mother used to hold me, God.
When I was hurt in spirit or flesh
She would gather me close
Stroke my silky hair and caress
My back with her warm hands.
Oh, God, I'm so lonely!

I remember the first boy who ever kissed me.
We were both so new at that.
The taste of young lips and popcorn,
The feeling deep inside of mysteries to come.
I remember Hank and the babies.
How can I remember them but together?
Out of the fumbling, awkward attempts of new lovers
Came the babies.
And as they grew, so did our love.

And, God, Hank didn't seem to care if my body thickened
And faded a little.
He still loved it,
And touched it.
And we didn't mind if we were no longer "beautiful."
And the children hugged me a lot.
Oh, God, I'm lonely!
Why didn't we raise the kids to be silly and affectionate?
As well as dignified and proper?
You see, they do their duty.
They drive up in their fine cars.
They come to my room and pay their respects.
They chatter brightly
And reminisce.
But they don't touch me.

They call me "Mom" or "Grandma"
Never Minnie.
My mother called me Minnie.
And my friends.
Hank called me Minnie, too.
But they're gone.
And so is Minnie.
Only Grandma is here.
And, God! She is lonely![5]

No medicine or counseling or religious service can cure Minnie's problem. She needs to be touched and caressed and called by name. This is true for all of us. Where medicine fails, touch and its accompanying powers often work.

Enjoying Your Body

In the beginning of his ministry, St. Francis of Assisi called his body "brother ass." As he moved among the sick, the lepers, and the poor, he resented the time required to feed and rest and clothe and care for his body. But an older and wiser St. Francis realized that his body was not some burdensome thing he must drag through life. A mature St. Francis called his body "brother friend."

But it seems to me there is a dimension beyond even the understanding of the body that St. Francis came to in his own maturity. A surgeon, of all people, has just written a book that celebrates the body. Dr. Richard Selzer is a surgeon-poet. Listen to his mini-essay on the skin: "I sing of the skin, layered fine as baklava, whose colors shame the dawn, at once the scabbard upon which is writ our only signature, and the instrument by which we are thrilled, protected, and kept constant in our natural place. Here is each man bagged and trussed in perfect amiability. See how it upholsters the bone and muscle underneath, now accenting the point of an elbow, now rolling over the pectorals to hollow the grotto of an armpit. Nippled and umbilicated, and perforated by the most diverse and marvelous openings, each with its singular rim and curtain."[6]

Levels of Reconciliation

Through Jesus Christ's life, death, and resurrection, we have the opportunity to be reconciled to God himself, to ourselves, to our brothers and sisters in the human family, and even to nature, both global and cosmic.

Now reconciliation can be experienced at many levels. If my enemy hates me and I him, the first level of reconciliation may simply be the cessation of hostilities. We can move from that to an armed truce and then an unarmed peace. But peace is only the prelude to the possibility of wishing my former enemy well and working for good on his behalf. Beyond that there is true love through which he becomes my friend and I learn to enjoy him and celebrate our relationship of love. This is ultimate reconciliation—and the goal of all life.

God's plan to reconcile me in all things and all relationships includes my relationship to my own body as well. I can move from hating and despising and being ashamed of my body to making peace with it. Cooperation with a former enemy and respecting him as a teacher is a giant step forward and the mark of true spirituality. But it is a far cry from liking, loving, and enjoying him—yea, celebrating him as one of God's good gifts to me. Wholeness ripens in the area of the physical, when I can truly love my body as a gift of God, for in reality, I am my body and my body is me. In other relationships, real love does not diminish with old age and failing faculties. It grows and deepens as new treasures are discovered. So might we love our physical selves.

Chapter 11

Find Your Place and Your People

To what extent can we shape, control, and enhance our environment? And to what extent are we helpless victims? Finding *your* place and *your* people is certainly one of the crucial issues in personal growth toward wholeness. Hazel and I used to feel very strongly that a change in environment doesn't change people until an incident some years ago made us reevaluate our thinking.

A third grade teacher had taken a dislike to one of our children. Her contempt was communicated to the entire class, and that year in school was a miserable one for our third grader. To live in an environment of nonaffirmation from teachers and peers is a killing experience. We prayed for

God to give our child the resources to transcend this negative environment and even to change it. Then one night my wife suggested that we could easily move across town to a new school district where our child would have a new environment and perhaps a new start. I was skeptical of this solution, but we decided to give it a try. During the next school year under a new teacher, one who seemed to genuinely love and enjoy this needy kid, we witnessed an academic and personal transformation.

Now I'm not suggesting that a new school guarantees a fresh start. New buildings do not make a new neighborhood. New or better housing does not automatically improve a family life racked by emotional and personality problems. But, on the other hand, all of us are strongly influenced by our environment. Our architectural, geographical, emotional, social, and spiritual surroundings are a tremendous shaping force.

The dream for a new environment has persisted throughout all time. In the past, nations have dreamed of enlarged empires. The Nazis dreamed of a world comprised solely of the Third Reich. Educators and philosophers dream of a convivial society—one with a greatly enhanced quality of life. Scientists and young people alike have a dream for a new environment produced by an ecological revolution which will return physical life on earth to its pristine state. And religious thinkers have always dreamed of a new order. Christians in particular believe that with the second coming of Jesus Christ there will be a new heaven and a new earth. And all of us dream of a new personal environment for ourselves or our loved ones—a place and a condition where we can achieve fulfillment and meaning.

Environment: Social, Cultural and Physical

A new concept was introduced to human thinking by Freud when he began to explore the subconscious forces which he believed controlled, motivated, and shaped people. But now we are discovering that man is not shaped totally by these inner forces, as Freud first thought. In part we are also shaped by the external forces around us.

Someone once said that trying to educate an individual without educating a society is like going off to find ivory. You must deal with the fact that there is an elephant attached. We all belong to groups and elephant-like institutions which have helped to make us the people we are. Jules Henry, author of *Pathways to Madness,* maintains that people go crazy not simply as individuals but as part of a group—usually the family group whose members unconsciously force that individual into a role and insist he live out that role.

But the external shaping forces are much wider than the family group. We are still living with a generation of people shaped largely by the mores of the Victorian era. A pre-World War II generation were the products of Andy Hardy, Shirley Temple, and the classic western with the clear delineation of good guys and bad guys. In each decade since then, young people have been uniquely shaped by their society; by the blandness of the fifties, by the revolt and unrest of the sixties, by the permissiveness of the seventies, marked by drugs and escapism. The society, different in each generation, is a shaping force whether you conform to its values or whether you choose to rebel.

But man is also influenced by his physical environment. For example, a study done in 1973 at the University of Pennsylvania proves conclusively that more people exhibit signs of depression when barometric pressure is higher than normal. But when the pressure drops, as it does before a storm, there is less depression and more intoxication and homicide. In fact there seems to be no limit to the varieties of forces in our environment which affect us and shape us.

In thinking of an ideal physical environment, we are the victims of the romantic myth that we can be more whole in the great wide open spaces than in the crowded cities. Thoreau is the patron saint of those who cling to this view. However, this idyllic dream is punctured by statistics which reveal that there is a higher rate of alcoholism, suicide, and mental illness in Montana, one of our least populated states, than there is in any of our crowded inner cities. However much people may "bug" us an environment which forces frequent interaction would seem to be the healthier one.[1]

Our culture, too, is an environmental factor in helping us become, for better or for worse, whatever we are. According to Dr. T. Glynn Williams of the Maryland Psychiatric Research Center, a good illustration of this idea is found in tribal life in places like New Guinea, where the native's identity is focused in tribal life. Survival of the tribe as opposed to personal survival represents the ultimate good, and one's personal death is not so important. Therefore, people within this tribal culture face death much more easily than we do in the Western world. Dr. Williams explained that our fear of death in his opinion dates back to the time of the Protestant Reformation with its emphasis on the worth of the individual as over against the good of society. If society is not necessarily of more worth than my individual life, then it is more difficult to come to grips with the fact that my life will end while society continues. Consciously or unconsciously, we feel that when we die, everything that matters to us dies. Dr. Williams claims that the theology of the Protestant Reformation has led us to believe that we are the center of God's creation. Any idea that life can end for us threatens us and makes us fearful.

Nevertheless, America today is becoming retribalized, according to Dr. Williams. We humans apparently have an unconscious longing for this kind of belonging. The communes, and other similar intimate communities, which are springing up represent an attempt to break society into subgroups as a means of sustaining our intense loyalties. Since patriotism as we have known it is no longer an "in" thing, the young have to create tribes to which they can belong and where their own loneliness and pain is minimized.

Environment and Mental Illness

We are also beginning to find a new appreciation of environment in the care of the emotionally or mentally disturbed. I believe it is safe to say that the majority of doctors practicing in mental hospitals today would agree that the environment within a psychiatric ward is often a great healing factor. Patients who feel lonely, estranged and without worth in their home environment, sometimes recover in a mental hospital because of the supportive, therapeutic society of fellow patients.

In a workshop at the Princeton Institute, R. D. Laing told a group of us the following story about the relatedness of environment and mental illness. As a young psychiatrist in England he worked in a large mental hospital and was assigned to a back ward for women, one where the "hopeless" ended up. Believing that this stark environment would hinder any return to emotional or psychic health, he had sixteen of the most seriously ill patients transferred to his care and moved them to a ward of their own. In this new facility, they had their own small kitchen and access to "sharp instruments" such as cooking knives and knitting needles. Within a year all sixteen women were released as "well." However, in checking on these women one year later, Dr. Laing found every one back once more in the mental hospital.

The implications seem clear. Rescued from the horror of the back wards and helped to function again, these women returned home to the same environment which had contributed to the original illness and they succumbed to that illness once again. There are lessons here, even for those of us not suffering from severe mental illness. If one is locked into a destructive situation where escape is impossible, then it is essential to arrange to have an environment if only for an hour a day or several hours a week that will help to promote healing and growth.

For example, a middle-aged woman I know was continuously being minimized and discounted by a husband who considered her dumb and ugly, when she was neither. She began to meet weekly with a small group of women in her church for fellowship, study and prayers. This loving, supportive climate enabled her to give up the tranquilizers and sleeping pills on which she had become dependent. She now sees that her husband's efforts to minimize her are really his problem.

The Educational Environment

Significant reappraisal is taking place in our educational environment. For example, studies are being made of the structure of school buildings. According to some experts, the egg crate arrangement of classrooms connected by long, echoing hallways reflects a concept of education dating from the late nineteenth century. In these buildings a lonely crowd moves along the hallway every forty minutes from one sterile classroom to another. The rooms have all the character of a waiting room in a bus depot. The new concept is to provide an environment which in addition to being a learning center is a place where students can intermingle socially with a sense of being and belonging. According to some pioneer educators, the new school building must provide students and teachers alike with a sense of having their own place—alone and separate from group pressures—to work and to discover and to assimilate knowledge. The schools without walls are one attempt at this kind of architecture.

But some of the most exciting things happening today are in teacher training which focuses on a new relational environment. At the University of Florida, Dr. Arthur Combs and his colleagues are doing a pioneer job in teacher training. Under their guidance a new breed of teachers is emerging. Prospective teachers are helped to see that impersonal remote learning does not produce students equipped to cope with the complexities of modern society. Here at the University of Florida they are seeking to provide a relational environment for their student teachers which will enable them to become the kind of people who can help their students to become whole.

A Shaping Force

Philosophers and historians have long been aware that our cultural environment creates and reflects our problems and needs. Almost thirty years ago Arnold Toynbee, recognizing that there are more dead cultures than live ones, gave us some guidelines about the conditions that prevail before the collapse of a culture in any period. These include a decreased sense of community and an increase in such signs of social sickness as: feelings of alienation and purposelessness, personal disorders and mental illness, the use of police to control behavior, the frequent and severe social disruptions, the acceptance of hedonistic behavior—to name a few.

But we have come a long way in the thirty years since Toynbee wrote that. We now see that environment is not just a barometer of man's corporate or personal condition, but a tool with which to shape his destiny. ARICA, one of the most eclectic and syncretistic of the new philosophies, defines the goal of human history in terms of producing a perfect society capable of producing perfect individuals.

How do we sort out the many kinds of environment which affect us and which become shaping forces in our growth and destiny? There are the immediate environmental factors such as the place where we live, the color of the walls, the quality of the air, and the noises or silences to which we are subjected. But perhaps some of the less obvious environmental factors are even more powerful. For example, the pace, priorities and patterns of our lives.

In *The One and Only You,* I reported on the town of Roseto, Pennsylvania, where sixteen hundred heavy eating Italians daily stuffed themselves with huge quantities of cholesterol-rich food but not a single person under forty-seven had ever had a heart attack. Suddenly that changed, and the heart attack rate in Roseto is now three times the national average even though younger people there are now eating less heart attack producing foods. But investigation indicates that the town has succumbed to "Americanization." There is competition and pressure and commuting and alienation as over against the closed, supportive environment that formerly characterized this little coal town with its European mores.

Overcoming a Negative Environment

But however negative the environment, there are people who do more than survive. They come through astoundingly intact psychically. Dr. Karl Menninger in a lecture to members of the American Psychiatric Association attributed this kind of survival to the presence of hope. He proposed that a deficiency of hope leads to decay and ultimately to our personal downfall. He cited cases of concentration camp inmates who survived not because of physical stature or strength or youth but because of an indefinable quality of hope.

Dr. Menninger went on to talk about helping patients to overcome a negative environment and how to give them hope. He says, "It is our responsibility as physicians to instigate some change in the relation of (the patient) to his environment—directly if possible, indirectly and gradually most likely. . . . By observing the internal and external processes we can discover what in his world is good for the patient and what is unbearable, what damage he inflicts upon himself and others, and what potentials within him remain underdeveloped. Here enters in hope, for we acquire, thus, a rationale for therapeutic intervention."[2] Dr. Menninger believes that all of us can have the inner resources to determine whether we live or die. If we can be helped to see ourselves "not as a mere spectator of cosmic events but as a prime mover . . . one important unit possessing the power to influence great decisions by making small ones."[3]

Since environment plays such an important role in each of our lives it seems imperative to learn to differentiate the positive and the negative, the healthy from the unhealthy environment, or the healing from the sickness producing environment. A study Dr. Menninger did in World War II in cooperation with the U.S. Army is a great help here. He was trying to determine the factor that created battle fatigue or nervous breakdown in battle and how to correct this. In that study he found the incidence of mental breakdown directly related to the kind of leadership in a particular unit.[4] All people are potentially capable of mental breakdown under stress, but the wrong kind of leadership can permit it to happen or even cause it to happen.

This would seem a strong reinforcement to those who believe man is innately good but corrupted by his environment. Yet, more recent tests show that mental breakdown can occur in an environmentless situation. Under controlled conditions where sensorally there is no environment, no weight, no sight, no smell, no sounds, no feelings, the subjects invariably go berserk. We are not made to live in an environmentless society.

The Need for Boundaries

To be whole and healthy our environment must have a boundary. This is true of people and organizations. It is impossible to conceive of a skinless man. The skin is a physical delineation of a person's ego and identity. Our environment is a continuous reminder of where we end and where the world begins. To be unclear about the boundary between ourselves and others is one definition of madness. The more romantically inclined may maintain that in a relationship of love they have entered into a fusion with someone else and are one with their mate or lover, but this is a fantasy and the beginning of madness. The boundary must exist to maintain integrity, personality, and sanity.

But, conversely, one can have too narrow a boundary. A creative experiment was conducted by Dr. John B. Calhoun for the National Institute for Mental Health. In his experiment which started in 1968 and ended in 1973, he placed four female and four male mice in an 8½′ x 8½′ environment with plenty of food and water, an ideal climate and no predators. The mice bred and formed social groups in which each animal found its role. Soon there were two hundred mice, four hundred, then over six hundred. There were no roles left within the little universe (which Calhoun likened to Spaceship Earth). Newcomers were then rejected and responded by attacking other mice viciously. Still the population grew to twenty-two hundred. By this time even females were uncharacteristically attacking others, even their own young. Young males did not learn to relate, to defend, to mate. Calhoun called them non-mice. The beautiful ones, physically perfect but unable to interact, huddled in a languid mass.

In their overcrowded city the mice learned to associate certain gratifying activities with the presence of others and to perform them only when others were close by. They packed themselves even closer together around food hoppers and water bottles. While some nesting boxes stood empty others were so crowded that mice suffocated. Reproduction ceased. As the months passed elders died and were not replaced. Calhoun said there was no hope. But the colony was allowed to follow its course in case someone thought there might be a rebirth when the population dropped back to the ideal size of one hundred and fifty. Finally, with no interference by man at all, the mouse population was reduced to one mouse, a female, and then she died.

Calhoun concluded that severe crowding for any species prevents its members from normal interaction and that eventually they are incapable of the kind of complex behavior development involved in things like reproduction or the defense of territory. For man, extreme overcrowding could prevent the development of acquisitional skills or of the ability to use ideas.[5] To me, this is an intriguing and somewhat frightening commentary on the effect of an overcrowded environment.

Finding a Friendly Environment—From Birth to Old Age

Our environment begins to affect us from birth and before. R. D. Laing claims the newborn baby's environment immediately begins to produce a sense of wrong identity, worthlessness and hopelessness. Laing says the modern hospital is a place for the ill and the dying and makes a very poor birthplace. "The mother is subjected to treatment by strangers; to the humiliating and unnecessary shaving of pubic hair, usually with a blunt razor. The first impact of the world is the hospital smell, the hospital sounds, the hospital air—the touch of unfriendly rubber gloves. The first breath is undoubtedly taken out of terror instead of coming naturally."[6]

It is difficult to pinpoint what constitutes a friendly environment because it varies for each of us. Anyone who has lived in a large family can attest to this. Some members prefer a cluttered and eternally messy room. To enforce neatness and order is to rob them of the environment they need at that time to grow, survive or prosper. At the other end of the scale are the aesthetics, so finely tuned to beauty and order that the wrong shade of wallpaper or an imperfect floral arrangement drives them wild. It is impossible to construct an ideal home just because of this limitless range of what is optimal or destructive for each one.

A study was undertaken at the Grace Hospital in New Haven to determine what kind of physical environment was maximum in helping people recover from nervous breakdowns. They were unable to arrive at any conclusion. Some people are greatly helped by living in a ward intimately surrounded by people all the time. In this cheek-to-jowl relationship they apparently receive their identity, their affirmation, and support for recovery. Others become sicker in this close environment and improve in private rooms with much solitary time and a chance to control their own environment.

But there are some positive ingredients we can look for in our environment which are genuinely healing and encourage growth for most people in most situations, though not in terms of geography, climate, or the aesthetic. One is that mysterious sense of "feeling at home," a condition arrived at so differently for each of us.

There are many of us who like to live in a place where we have sunk our roots and even where our ancestors have lived and died before us. Home is not just where I feel most like me. Home must be a place where I am surrounded by the familiar, whatever that may be. The important thing here is to help a person find out what "home" is for him. For the young and vigorous, home can be wherever one "feels at home" but as people grow older and more fixed in their ways, it is somehow even more important to be surrounded by the familiar.

To take an older person out of his home and neighborhood, away from family and familiar friends, and put him into a hospital where all is strange and unfamiliar results in the disorientation that is associated with senile psychosis. It is no wonder that people like this get lost and wander around the halls urinating in broom closets. They literally don't know where the bathroom is. A borderline senile psychosis blossoms into a full scale one because the human mechanism simply cannot handle that kind of change in environment.

A Relational Environment

Another generally therapeutic dimension of a good environment involves being able to relate in small groups. Not all small groups are good climates in which to grow, but it would seem that we need to belong to some kind of micro family for maximum growth. It is not healthy to live one's life apart from belonging intimately to a few people. In belonging intimately to a few others behavior has a chance of changing.

Here's what Nancy Smith in her book *Journey Out of Nowhere* says about the needs of those leaving the mental hospital: "First the patient needs to feel welcome in his own home and neighborhood. It is true that others have had to assume his responsibilities for months or even years, but they must willingly step down now and give the patient the opportunity to prove himself. A father must have the chance of eventually resuming being the head of the house. The mother will have to manage the household and rear her children.

"Small, 'busy' jobs are not enough. A man who once earned twenty thousand dollars a year will not feel he is carrying his share of the load by taking out the garbage. He may begin with the easy household tasks, but don't hold him there and don't praise him for this simple job by gushing, 'Good boy,' as if he were a well trained dog.'"[7]

She is talking about being a responsible member of a small group as a follow-up to any good institutionalized care. But for maximum growth we all need this climate of belonging to a group where our behavior is observed and where we are accountable for our share of the load.

Let's be realistic about the available options for choosing a relational environment. Suppose your problem is that you are seriously overweight. One choice you have is to withdraw from society, living in your own fantasy world and continuing to overeat. Apparently many overweight people do become loners and have primarily themselves for company. Another choice is to become somewhat paranoid about your problem. Acting out of your own frustration or resentment, you are belligerent in your encounters with others. A third option might be to become the stereotype "jolly fat person" who makes friends everywhere, seeking sympathy. If you claim you are the helpless victim of your "glands," your many friends are happy to confirm this self diagnosis. But a fourth option is to join a group of people who have a similar problem. No quick sympathy here. Negative behavior is pointed out and a positive course of action outlined. Members help each other in a common therapeutic program.

Whether the problem is overweight or terminal cancer, we have the same obvious options for choosing a relational environment. One such support group for terminal cancer patients meets in an office building in Washington, D.C., every Monday evening. They meet together to find sustenance and support from one another. They recount their fears, angers, dreads and they can speak without embarrassment or shame. They can openly discuss suicide but few seem to consider it. Their bond is not death but life in the face of death. They give hope to one another to make the most of whatever time they have left and, I would add, that by so doing it is quite likely their lives are being prolonged.[8]

Making Choices

Surely the crucial question is how do we go about trying to build the ideal environment for growth for ourselves and those we love? To what extent can we control environment and to what extent can we learn to live with that part of the environment we cannot control? The most profound answer is in the classic Alcoholics Anonymous prayer, "Lord, help me to change those things that I can change; to accept those things that I cannot change; and the wisdom to know one from the other." For if we endure with resignation a destructive environment which could be changed, we are both pathetic and foolish. But to rebel against an environment that is unchangeable is childish, destructive, and fruitless.

I know a lovely woman in her early fifties who is a widow of considerable means. She lives in a town with her brothers and sisters and their families, and they are all involved in a business together. The family is excessively protective and tend to treat her like the family dumbbell. They told her when to sign papers or how to vote her stock. For her the whole experience was demeaning and minimizing. We talked at some length about why she remained in that town. She is gifted, bright, and beautiful. We talked about the possibility of changing her social environment by moving to another town where she might be more appreciated as a person. Obviously, the decision was not an easy one. She could stay in a place which was sentimentally pleasing with many memories of places and events shared with husband and parents, all now dead, and put up with bad vibes from her family. Or she could move to the uncertainty of a new place in the hope of finding people who would genuinely appreciate her for the warm and gifted person she is.

Because of her financial independence she was able to make the move, but there are many others who are trapped in a job or economic situation without the same freedom. And as long as there are trapped people in the world it must be of concern to me as a fellow human and as a Christian. I must become my brother's brother and help him become free from the pressures that bind him. All social service is in a large part self serving. No one can live in a crushing environment anywhere in the world without affecting me, directly or indirectly, in some way.

During my research, I visited one of R. D. Laing's homes for the mentally ill in London. These are places where people can find relief from the pressures of family or society. They provide an alternative to the usual mental hospital. But Laing's dream is even larger. "All of society," he says, "ought to be an asylum for the people who comprise it. That's what a decent society would be like, isn't it?"

Chapter 12

The Day of the Amateur

Perhaps the most exciting single development on the horizon for changing life as we know it is what I like to call the resource revolution. In my judgment this revolution will be as radical as the physical resource revolution of the future where atomic or solar power will replace gas, coal, oil or wood.

The resource revolution will bring about a whole new approach for finding, recruiting, training, equipping, and enabling nonprofessional people to minister to each other in all of the helping and learning professions. And this need is critical because of the tragic shortage of personnel and funds in the major helping professions. How can this shortage be alleviated? Where are the para-professionals who can be trained and equipped to fill the vacuum in institutions, schools, jails and social service organizations?

Quite frankly, I think they will come from people just like you and me. For example, in spite of our busyness we have more leisure time than any other society in history. Senior citizens have no outlets for a lifetime of experience. Young people in increasing numbers are simply unemployed. The middle class is faced with extended leisure and a shrinking work week. All of these groups are resources to be tapped. Certainly, with our growing recognition of social responsibility and with our increased awareness that personal growth and fulfillment comes in helping others, there should be a vast reservoir of raw talent with time and willingness to learn. And there seems ample evidence to suggest that in many cases the ordinary untrained para-professional can be as effective in ministering to the needs of others as his highly trained expensive professional counterpart.

Education and the Para-professional

A new day seems to be dawning in that all-important field of education. This is beautifully exemplified at the Beacon Hill Free School of Boston. Here more than two thousand students, ranging in age from five to seventy-five, have enrolled in hundreds of courses. A wide variety of subjects are offered—from the three R's to yoga, indoor gardening, ecology, pollution, belly dancing, foreign languages, and crocheting. The school owns no property. No one pays to attend class and no one is paid to teach. The yearly budget is estimated at under a hundred dollars and that is mainly for postage. All teaching, secretarial, and administrative services are volunteered. Students receive no credits. An environment is provided and those who want to learn and those who want to teach are brought together.

A similar school, Communitas, in Washington, D.C., has only eleven students. It is the smallest college in the country and one of the most unusual. Here, students design their own program of study and then launch out for the year on a learning pilgrimage. A small staff gives guidance, but the student selects an expert from the field of his particular interest and they work together as student-teacher-adviser throughout the year. It is a reminder of the tutorial system of past years or even the apprenticeship system of the Middle Ages. Both of these schools are tapping non-professionals for the teaching role with good results.

Even in more staid learning centers, a more relational style of teaching is replacing some of our former content-centered methods. Dr. Combs of the University of Florida in Gainesville insists there is no right or good method for teaching or for training teachers. Rather, the key in education is a spontaneous and instantaneous response to a person. In other words, self is the essential instrument in teaching. The analogy he uses in his seminars is that you don't learn to doctor, you become a doctor. You don't learn to teach, you learn how to become a teacher. The teacher uses his or her life as an enabling process through spontaneity and instantaneous response to help another learn.

Dr. Morrell Klute of Wayne State University in Detroit believes that no one ever teaches another human being. Instead, every individual teaches himself. He further believes that it is a fallacy to think that one person can be trained to teach a subject to another person. If, as Klute says, every person teaches himself, this modifies our understanding of the role of the teacher and opens the door for the extended use of the para-professional on the educational scene.

Psychiatry and the Para-professional

The field of psychiatry is perhaps even more vulnerable to the premise that the para-professional can be a valid and capable resource for those with "mental problems." Decades ago, as Sigmund Freud developed psychoanalysis, he said, "The internal development of psychoanalysis is everywhere proceeding, contrary to my intentions, away from lay analysis and becoming a pure medical specialty and I regard this as fatal for the future of analysis."[1]

Dr. E. Fuller Torrey, a Washington psychiatrist, has written a book called *The Death of Psychiatry* in which he outlines two reasons for this "death." One is that recent extensive research indicates that non-medically trained people—social workers, nurses and psychologists—are doing just as good a job as the medically trained psychiatrist with his long term analysis. Secondly, the most common mental illnesses, such as schizophrenia and depression, respond better to drugs than to psychiatry.

Listen to his prognosis for current psychiatrists: "Those of us who are currently psychiatrists, who have chosen a profession which is going the route of the platypus, will have to make a choice. Either we can return to neurology and treat people with true brain disease or we can become tutors—educators—counselors who teach people about themselves and how to solve their problems. In the first instance we would probably have to work harder . . . and in the second instance we would make less money."

Torrey believes that most of the people now being treated as mentally ill should be seen for what they are—people with problems. He says, "They may need help in solving them. But there is nothing wrong with their minds. They have no illness. They're like the rest of us with problems, only theirs may be bigger and more difficult to cope with. The non-medical therapist, many of whom have now begun private practices of their own, are helping them as well as anyone can."[2]

"Love . . . is nature's psychotherapy," says psychiatrist Eric Berne in his book *What Do You Say After You Say Hello?*[3] If he is correct, then that kind of psychotherapy is in no way limited to the professionals.

Medicine and the Para-professional

In the field of medicine the use of the para-professional in the armed services has long been a common practice. As a sergeant in combat during World War II, I have my own vivid recollections of the aid man or corpsman. He was an enlisted man who fought with us, marched with us, lived with us. He was our first line of medical aid; he treated gunshot wounds, shrapnel wounds, shock, or any other kind of medical problem, including the common cold.

In the People's Republic of China, they have adopted this live-in medic idea and applied it to their civilian life with impressive results. To deliver medical services to greater numbers of people and in remote places, a daring experiment is being tried. Indigenous para-professionals are trained for short intensive times and put to work while on the job training continues. These para-professional medics work to bring healing to those around them while functioning in their primary roles as factory workers, housewives, and peasant farmers. These healers are not a separate professional caste. With today's escalating costs, we will surely have to find new ways to meet our own nation's increased medical needs. Perhaps a civilian version of the corpsman could be part of the solution.

The Church: A Recruiting Agency for the Para-professional

The church seems a logical place to both train and recruit the para-professional to serve and assist in any number of areas. In a recent poll by the American Medical Association, as I mentioned earlier in another chapter, it has been suggested that at least ninety percent of the people who visit a doctor's office in a day actually have "life" problems rather than medical ones. Lacking time to give an hour of listening and caring to twenty-five different patients, doctors are forced instead to prescribe tranquillizers. How can we implement the recruiting and training of para-professionals by the church to meet this great need, a need recognized by the doctors themselves?

In New Testament times every believer was called to be a priest—part of a royal priesthood. The ministry was not restricted to those professionally trained. Fuller Theological

Seminary in Pasadena, California, offers a course which embodies this new approach to ministry. Here is how they describe it: "Changing times and the crisis in congregational life calls for creative new approaches to theological education. Increasingly, the expanding religious movements of today are led by the laity. The theological education and training of the laity is essential for the vitality and growth of the church in our times. Seminaries traditionally do not provide theological training for lay persons. Therefore, it is essential for the future of the church that theological training of the highest quality be provided for those persons engaged in secular professions who desire to expand their abilities for Christian service."

These extension ministries at Fuller Seminary are not geared for those leaving secular vocations to become clergymen. Rather, it is their contention that an authentic call to ministries of healing and helping has essentially nothing to do with being a "professional."

There is nothing new about this emphasis on the priesthood of all believers—for every believer is called to be a priest to his fellowman. This doctrine, stated clearly in the New Testament, was rediscovered by Luther and the Protestant Reformers and is now embraced heartily by the Roman Catholic church as well.

But the revolutionary dimension of this spiritual truth in our times is the focus of the priesthood on the world, rather than exclusively on fellow believers. If we believe that every Christian is called to be a priest of healing and liberation in all of society, then they can be helped and trained to minister to each other in the helping and learning professions. Believers can be trained and recruited to help harried and over-worked doctors, educators, social workers, psychiatrists and counselors, with their work.

In the Book of Acts we find non-Christians looking to those in the early church as a source of healing. As a matter of fact, in its public relations, this was the earliest image projected by the church of Christ. Using a strategy of pre-evangelism or prevenient grace, the Holy Spirit in those early years healed and helped the world through believers.

If we recapture that basic strategy, then the church of Jesus Christ, through its laity, may once again become salt, leaven and light to a needy world.

Counseling and the Para-professional

In training people for this kind of para-professional service in any of the areas we've mentioned, it seems that we must first of all raise their level of confidence. Without years of schooling in education, psychiatry, counseling, how can we expect to help others effectively on some sort of one-to-one basis?

In 1955 I did graduate work in psychology at Boston University and my major paper was on the work of F. E. Fiedler, who in the late 1940s did research on the effectiveness of various schools of psychology and psychiatry. His studies advanced the hypothesis now held by many leading psychiatrists and psychologists that the therapist's attitude toward his patient, and not his theory or technique, is the factor that makes counseling effective. Hence, it would seem that the therapeutic element common to all counseling is the counseling relationship itself, and the key to an effective relationship is the proper attitude on the part of the counselor. The studies proved that these attitudes which produced therapeutic relationships were nontransferable in the classroom. So we are talking about something beyond the academic. Apparently there are innate attitudes and qualities which enable some counselors to be a healing force in the life of another. It is not difficult to make the transition then to the fact that lay people with these same innate gifts can cultivate them to an extent that will enable them to be therapists and counselors. Fiedler's studies seem to indicate that the therapist's ability to enter into a meaningful relationship with his counselee is the factor which promotes healing. This is good news for the concerned, untrained person who wants to help another.

A Common Sense Approach

Well, if this resource revolution is a reality, what must we believe and do to be a part of this para-professional force to help and heal others? First, we must rid ourselves of the feeling that therapeutic techniques are all part of some esoteric mystique; that we must learn complicated theories of personality and methods to recognize and deal with a variety of mental and emotional problems difficult to analyze or cure. The Copernican thinkers in psychotherapy are those who have taken a common sense approach to what makes people hurt. One of the most articulate and radical spokesmen for this common sense approach is William Glasser. Here are six areas in which he takes issue with conventional psychotherapy:[8]

1. His denial that there is such a thing as mental illness. He believes people are responsible for their behavior. This is in contrast to conventional psychiatry which believes mental illness can be meaningfully classified and treated according to diagnostic classification.

2. His refusal to get involved with the patient's history. Glasser works in the present and toward the future because the patient cannot change what has happened to him. Conventional psychiatrists probe into the patient's past life believing that with an understanding of his psychological roots, the patient can change his attitude toward life.

3. The use of a reality relationship. Glasser relates to his patients as himself, not as a transference figure. The conventional therapist uses transference to help the patient relive past difficulties and then points out that the same inadequate behavior is being repeated with the therapist.

4. His refusal to allow the patient to excuse his behavior on the basis of unconscious motivations. Glasser considers

unconscious conflicts or the reason for them unimportant. Conventional psychiatry considers unconscious mental conflicts more important than conscious problems. The patient is made aware of these unconscious conflicts, through free association, interpretation of transference and of dreams.

5. His emphasis on moral behavior. Glasser faces the issue of right and wrong with his patients convinced this solidifies the involvement. In conventional psychiatry, deviant behavior is the product of mental illness and the patient isn't morally responsible because he isn't able to behave differently.

6. His concern with helping the patient find more satisfactory patterns of behavior. Conventional psychiatric therapy is not concerned with promoting better behavior, contending that behavior will improve once the historical and unconscious sources of the problem are understood.

Glasser's point of view represents those of a great many innovative therapists in the field and opens the door for the para-professional. He punctures the myths which have hampered the ordinary person from feeling adequate to deal with someone else's problems. If Glasser is correct, then anyone with average ability and intellect and sensitivity can risk becoming involved with a fellow human who is struggling with a personal problem.

Recently I asked Paul Tournier how he counsels people. He said, "I am very embarrassed by all these people who ask me that. I don't know how to help people. I don't do anything at all. What is important is that the people try to find their way and that I try to understand, to support them, to welcome them. What is important is that people find me a true friend, someone in whom they confide everything. That is the most magnificent thing to see. What a privilege to find someone in whom you can confide without fear of being judged."

The kind of relationship Tournier speaks about is open to anyone willing to be a friend and pay the price of friendship. But although extensive professional training is not necessary to be effective in the resource revolution, nevertheless there are certain very helpful basic skills in a relationship that we can learn. Gerald Goodman identifies three of them and calls them the "therapeutic triad": "Understanding (empathy), openness (self-disclosure), and acceptance-warmth, which combine to form a therapeutic talent composite."[5] Thomas Oden in his book *Game Free* cites a great many studies beyond Goodman's to prove that people with these three abilities are tremendously effective with other people.[6] Incidentally, those who do not have them are unable to help a counselee in any measurable way, no matter how well trained professionally.

The Source of All Healing

Finally, to take our place as para-professionals we need to reckon with the fact that healing is a mysterious process instigated by God. There is an old maxim I've heard many doctors quote reverently, "I only change the bandages, God heals the wounds." This is just as true with mental and emotional healing. In the counseling situation, there is a third force that can be relied upon to break through and do the unexpected because we expect Him to.

In 1942, Karl Menninger said, "Love is the medicine for the sickness of the world." Love is too big to be encompassed; love is theological, love is personal, love is doing more than feeling. But whatever else love is, it has no strings and it does not make others dependent on us. Love is not doing for others. Love is not becoming your brother's keeper. Love is being your brother's brother; to help him to find his own resources, his dignity, his strength and his non-dependence.

This is the day of the para-professional—the day of the layman priest. God has called his church to be a royal priesthood; every believer is a priest, and a priest is one who mediates strength and grace and healing from God to people.

Buried deep in the mystery of our humanity is the priceless treasure of our ordinariness. All of us ordinary people with our ordinary crushing problems can often be helped best by other ordinary people. We learn from role models at every stage of our life and models must be those with whom we can identify—those persons who are not frightening and who, in turn, are not frightened of us. This is the meaning—and certainly the mystery—of the human condition. It is life shared. Today I hurt and need you. Tomorrow you hurt and need me. Profound and simple. Simply profound. The priesthood of all believers—God's dream for us.

One final bit of research seems to illuminate this point most whimsically. At the University of Wisconsin's Regional Primate Research Center Dr. Stephen Suomi, Dr. Harry Harlow and Dr. William McKenny were working with psychotic monkeys, monkeys who had become psychotic because they were deprived of their mothers and isolated for the first month of their lives. They tried many methods to help the monkeys overcome their psychosis. The only thing that worked was exposure to very young monkeys—monkeys who had not yet learned monkey behavior. These young monkeys, "untrained" by life, proved to be perfect therapists. On the other hand, monkeys the same age or older than the psychotic monkeys had already learned such set ways of behavior that they could not relate to the sick ones. How fortunate that there are so many of us untrained monkeys around in the school of life.

Chapter 13

Where Does It Hurt?

A gifted counselor I know deals with people who come to see him by asking two basic questions. "What do you really want and what do you have to do to get it?" His results are impressive, but it seems to me there is a problem in this approach. Part of the meaning and mystery of being human is that we are often very obtuse about perceiving what it is we really want. And even knowing that, we tend to take some pretty unconstructive routes to getting what we want. This kind of a diagnosis requires a good deal of objectivity and insight and is often difficult to arrive at alone.

And yet in other areas, all of us are diagnosticians every day. A housewife confronted with a culinary failure must diagnose her problem by rechecking the original recipe. The salesman who would be successful needs to diagnose what went wrong in every lost sale. When a business is losing money, a study must be made of production costs, the desirability of the product, distribution, sales, advertising, and so on.

So, too, in all the scientific fields dealing with human growth and potential, accurate diagnosis is often the difference between success or failure. Perhaps this is why the diagnostician, at least in the medical sciences, demands such great respect and high salaries.

The resources available to the medical practitioner are of little use if he cannot arrive at the accurate diagnosis of the patient's problem. Every successful psychiatrist or psychological counselor has an explicit or implicit hope for each patient or client who comes to see him. The ever increasing technical and psychological resources being developed to help people to learn are of little avail if the classroom teacher cannot diagnose particular needs and apply whatever resources are necessary to enable a non-learner or slow learner to improve.

Some Creative Diagnostic Approaches

In the field of education, the Oakland Community College, Oakland, California, has been using computers to analyze the cognitive style best suited to each student. Some learn best in a family setting with much group interaction. Others learn better independently. Some independent learners retain more through visual rather than auditory input. By making use of no less than thirteen different learning environments, they have reduced failures from a constant 37% to 3%.

In Baltimore County, Maryland, law officers are using a new kind of diagnosis to control traffic accidents. Johns Hopkins School of Medicine researchers studied the deaths of fifty male drivers killed over a four year period in the county. Close friends and relatives of the victims were asked to rate the men in eighteen categories of social behavior. Researchers then compared these scores with those of a random group.

Findings indicated that auto fatality victims are usually more belligerent, talkative, negative and hyperactive.

Psychologist Margaret Naumberg is using an unusual diagnostic device in the marriage counseling situation. Basing her therapy on the common psychoanalytic theory that individuals frequently suffer from unconscious conflicts, she asks each marriage partner to draw a picture of the marriage. From their drawings she is able to uncover important hidden feelings and attitudes. The marriage from one spouse's point of view is non-verbally illustrated to the other partner and to the therapist, providing a freer avenue of communication to those who have difficulty in the verbal dimension. The counselee is free to make his own diagnosis of the problem which is then interpreted by the therapist.

Tom Szasz is well known for his conviction that basic diagnosis is the cause of much that is wrong in the treatment of the mentally ill. In October 1971 the *New York Times Magazine* reported a verbatim interview of Dr. Szasz helping his students diagnose a patient. Here are some excerpts from that interview:

> At New York State University's Upstate Medical Center, a routine diagnostic interview is in progress. The patient . . . had been complaining of a mysterious "pulling in her head." In a flat voice she unfolds a story . . . filled with disaster, loss and sudden death.
>
> "Well, what is your diagnosis?" Szasz asks, turning to [the students] after the patient has been escorted from the room. "Come now," he prods ironically. "You are the *doctors* and she is the *patient*, so that means there must be an *illness*. Otherwise we wouldn't all be here, would we?"
>
> "I think," ventures a young man with a sprouting blonde beard, "That she is in a chronic depression."
>
> "I think," [says another student] "that potentially it's a case of involutional melancholia. But for right now, I guess I'd concur in a diagnosis of chronic, severe depression."
>
> Szasz looks at him with interest: "And then how would you go about treating this 'condition'?"

There is a pause. "Rrr . . . isn't there a drug called Elavil that's good for depression?"

The psychiatrist blinks several times parodying extreme amazement: "So you would treat this 'sickness' she's got with *drugs?* . . . but what, exactly, are you treating? Is feeling miserable—needing someone to talk things over with—a form of medical *illness?*" Szasz gets to his feet, walks over to a blackboard and picks up a piece of chalk.

He turns and writes in large block letters: "DEPRESSION." And underneath that: "UNHAPPY HUMAN BEING." "Tell me," he says facing the class, "Does the psychiatric term say more than the simple descriptive phrase? Does it do anything other than turn a person with problems into a patient with a sickness?"

Whether the problem is a failed marriage, repeated traffic accidents, a learning disability or being an unhappy human being, there is new hope on the human scene. Rather than redoubling their efforts to bring solutions, these innovative groups and individuals are attempting a fresh diagnosis of old problems.

"The Barnum Effect"

Sometimes our needs may be diagnosed accurately and yet in such general terms as to not be particularly helpful. Perhaps you are one of the millions of people who read your horoscope in the newspaper each day. I'll venture a guess that you're often struck, as I am, by the accuracy of that particular reading. But, on second thought, most of the suggestions or predictions would apply to anyone at any time. We have probably all been impressed at some point by prophetic statements from some spiritual or astrological seer, statements like: "You have some unresolved conflicts dating back to your childhood." "You've never really tapped your full potential." "You have a fear that others may not like you." "You are very critical of yourself." Actually, all of these are a pretty accurate diagnosis of the general human condition.

A Dr. Bertram Forer gave thirty-nine students what he calls

the Diagnostic Interest Blank Test, and he promised to provide a personality evaluation for each student based on the results. A week later he handed out the following personality sketch to every single one of the students, taking precautions that no one could see another sketch. All thirty-nine read this identical personality evaluation:

1. You have a great need for other people to like and admire you.
2. You have a tendency to be critical of yourself.
3. You have a great deal of unused capacity which you have not turned to your advantage.
4. While you have some personality weaknesses, you are generally able to compensate for them.
5. Your sexual adjustment has presented problems for you.
6. Disciplined and self-controlled outside you tend to be worrisome and insecure inside.
7. At times you have serious doubts as to whether you have made the right decision or done the right thing.
8. You prefer a certain amount of change and variety and become dissatisfied when hemmed in by restrictions and limitations.
9. You pride yourself as an independent thinker and do not accept other's statements without satisfactory proof.
10. You have found it unwise to be too frank in revealing yourself to others.
11. At times you are extroverted, affable, sociable; while other times you are introverted, wary, reserved.
12. Some of your aspirations tend to be pretty unrealistic.
13. Security is one of your major goals in life.

Students were asked to rate on a scale of 0 (poor) to 5 (perfect) how effectively the test revealed their own personality. All but one student rated the test with a grade of 4 or 5. The one exception graded it as a 3. After the papers were handed in the students were asked to raise their hand if they felt the test had rated them accurately. Almost every hand went up. Dr. Forer then read the first item on the personality sketch and asked if anyone had found anything similar on his sketch. When every hand went up, the class burst into laughter. He then pointed out that the experiment had been performed simply to demonstrate our tendency to be overly impressed by vague statements and to endow the diagnostician with an unwarrantedly high degree of insight.[1]

Dr. Paul E. Meehl, in writing about this tendency, said that his colleagues call it the Barnum Effect, "a personality description after the manner of P. T. Barnum."[2]

The Barnum Effect must be taken into account in any diagnostic procedure. When the church diagnoses man's problems, it can also be guilty of generalities so vague (though true!) as to be virtually meaningless. For example, the church diagnoses man's problem as "sin" for which the solution is "grace," and while this is certainly sound, it isn't especially helpful. The early church as described in the New Testament tried to deal with sin in its particulars—lust, envy, drunkenness, resentment—rather than with the universal and general "sin." I would hope that the church in our time could once again deal with life specifically and help people today deal with these same basic human difficulties.

The Place of Diagnosis in Personal Growth: Some Options

Whether we are diagnosing emotional, physical, mental, educational or relational problems, all diagnostic attempts seem to fall into three very distinct categories. First of all, there is the diagnosis based on some source apart from the patient or seeker. This outside source of diagnosis might be a therapist, a school of thought, a test, or even a technical device such as a computer. The basic assumption here is that we can trust someone or something to diagnose our needs. Second, there is the diagnosis we can arrive at on our own. Self evaluation and insight can come through meditation, studying, reading or participation in a group process. But, fundamentally we diagnose our own needs and set our own course for growth. A third and quite distinctive approach to diagnosis is what we might call mutual diagnosis. In mutual diagnosis, two or more people, non-professionals, are reflectors of each other's needs. Each is equally involved in growth or therapy, each is accountable to the other, and each provides the other with an objective look at the problems.

If we are embarking on a course for personal growth, diagnosis from an outside source is probably the most familiar approach. Certainly there are some sensitive and gifted counselors and therapists able to do an outstanding job with this kind of diagnosis. But, unfortunately, gifted counselors are in very short supply. Another problem is that relying on diagnosis from an outside source seems to contradict the ultimate goal of most therapy which Fritz Perls defines this way: "What we are after is the maturation of the person, removing the blocks that prevent a person from standing on his own feet. We try to help him make the transition from environmental support to self support."[3]

Personal growth through self-diagnosis is the approach used generally in the church. A smorgasbord of opportunities is available to most church members and the average churchgoer is expected by intuition or prayer to determine his own needs and to program himself for necessary courses of study.

But, some years ago I came to the conclusion that self diagnosis is not too reliable. I had devised a type of self diagnosis test for the members of some small groups in which I was involved to determine each person's growing edge. Consistently, people who seemed to be highly motivated and approaching actualization rated themselves much lower than those who were more obviously troubled, unmotivated and poor achievers. This experience seemed to demonstrate for me how difficult it is to effectively evaluate ourselves.

Part of our problem is that we tend to do the things that we have always done and in which we feel comfortable. The Bible study group member never joins a picket line. The socially concerned protestor, though a Christian, wouldn't dream of attending a prayer meeting. In the physical realm, a group of doctors are presently researching why the body tends to encourage cancer cells while it rejects life saving organ transplants. The only explanation to date is that the body seems to feed and encourage the familiar while it fears and rejects the strange. Cancer cells are given extra blood supplies while a new organ is strange and therefore rejected. Apparently we have the same problem in the psychic and spiritual realms. I instinctively fear and withdraw from the very things I need for health and balance and I pursue those things which increase my psychic and spiritual imbalance.

Personal Growth through Mutual Diagnosis

I personally believe that the best avenue for personal growth is through what I would call mutual diagnosis. This is a diagnosis arrived at with the help of another, who is also a non-professional and who is himself seeking growth and wholeness.

Accountability plays a big part in this kind of mutual diagnosis. We have all heard often that behavior observed is behavior changed. Left to myself, I am more apt to act irresponsibly or dishonestly. I need someone else not primarily for answers but in order to be held accountable; someone who will hold me to the truth and to my commitments and who will not let me off the hook.

I mentioned earlier my visit to the private clinic near Baden Baden, Germany, for alcoholics and general neurotics, run by Walther Lechler, a German psychiatrist. Many staff members who have come there to work have since discovered their own needs and have become patients for a time. The clinic operates on the premise that each person needs to grow, the professionals as much as the guests. Beyond that, each patient is asked to diagnose his own condition before admission and to describe his expectations for his time at the clinic. Thereafter, each patient must submit a weekly progress evaluation to the staff. At staff meetings, the patient's own evaluation is read to give a more complete picture. A beautiful kind of mutuality seems to exist between professionals and those they are attempting to help.

I discussed this kind of mutual diagnosis with my friend Keith Miller, a gifted counselor and author of a number of best-selling books. He said, "Many people I talk to are bored with premature affluence or are experiencing male or female menopause. Maybe they have fulfilled their daddy's dream or their own dreams but what are they going to do with the rest of their lives? I don't really have any rules about how to help somebody. I try to be very sensitive about attempting to find out where a person is and then bringing whatever I have to that point. That may sound like a copout. I don't treat everybody the same way. Some people I can confront and with others I am passive and non-directive. I don't have any helping stance."

It seems to me that this is precisely the kind of helping stance any counselor not professionally trained can assume. If you can take time to find out where the other person is, or thinks he is, and where he wants to go, and what he wants to be and where he is hurting, you may establish a relationship which can provide the strength and help needed for growth.

Personal Growth: A Cooperative Effort

As I was writing this chapter I read about a woman in Louisville, Kentucky, who had a brain operation. Since she had been suffering from severe headaches all her life, a neurosurgeon performed a seventeen-hour operation on her brain. She was given a local anesthetic. For all seventeen hours, the patient was conscious and assisting in the operation. The staff could measure their progress by her ability or inability to function as directed. In the realm of the psychological or the spiritual, I would like to be like that patient. I don't want to be unconscious at the mercy of another, nor do I want to attempt my own "spiritual" brain surgery. If someone else will wield the knife or hold the mirror, I will cooperate in exploring my needs and finding healing and wholeness. It is my hope that as we begin to exercise this kind of mutual diagnosis we can learn from each other in a profound way the meaning and mystery of being human.

Perhaps the genius of the Christian Church, when it is truly the Church, is that it is a fellowship of priests, each caring for a few others and being accountable to those same others. Hence we avoid the pitfall of living in deadly isolation, accountable to no one and responsible only for ourselves and our own actions and decisions.

Many of us for too long have lived out the philosophy, "I am the master of my fate; I am the captain of my soul." Others, feeling ill-equipped for their autonomous and self-directed role, seek some outside authority who will prescribe their needs and dictate the cure. The great response to such authoritarian ministries in the church today points to the desperate need in many for outside authority. It seems that any authoritative Christian leader offering advice, however old and unsuitable, however clinically or theologically unsound and threadbare, or however new and untried and bizarre, can get a following of devoted, even fanatical followers.

But, to take seriously the priesthood of all believers dictates a middle course between these two alternatives. I believe that as Christians and churchmen our task is to care for people—listening, reflecting, questioning, but never robbing another of his own dignity and his need to choose responsibly his course of direction. We affirm that in the healing of souls, there is no one cure-all. Medicine must be administered on a personal basis. Self-administered medicine has limitations. We need the word of interpretation from another—from The Other—who has promised to live in all others who will allow it.

Jesus always diagnosed on a person-to-person basis. He suggested that the sin of Nicodemus was pride ("You must be born again!"). He diagnosed the rich young ruler's problem as greed ("Sell all that you have and give it to the poor!"). He dealt with the Samaritan woman's immorality ("Go call your husband . . . !"). Each person Jesus encountered had a next step in growth which was unique and personal. Those in whom the Great Physician lives can help us find our next step.

As a Christian, I believe that each person has been given by God the gift of discernment. This gift applies to our perception of the needs and growth potential of others. I believe this is the mystery and meaning behind the Christian concept that we are a race of priests. I need you and you need me. I can help you and you can help me. We are members one of another—never meant to live in isolation.

Chapter 14

Conclusions and New Directions

Experts in space travel tell us that we are successful in placing men and machines on the moon because of the incorporation of frequent on-course corrections. At various times and stages during the journey, computers calculate the distance covered and assay the spaceship's present position. And, on the basis of those conclusions, a revised course is plotted. Those same experts state that there are still so many unknown variables in celestial navigation that it is presently impossible to set a course from earth to moon with no corrections.

A quest for the meaning and mystery of human life must, as well, allow for many on-course corrections. That is why it is essential at this point for us to examine our course and what we feel has been discovered. This time of searching has been the most demanding and challenging period of my life. I have learned much from many brilliant and gracious people, and have visited many places where intriguing experiments in growth and healing are taking place.

Every journey, happy or unhappy, successful or unsuccessful, leaves its mark on the traveler. I am not the person I was at the beginning of my quest four years ago. I have seen, learned, observed, and experienced things about people and their potential that I must incorporate in any future programs aimed at facilitating personal growth. I am well aware that in time I will have discovered more and will have to enlarge or revise my conclusions. Most of these conclusions have already been the basis for an individual chapter and have been explored at much length, but for the sake of presenting the whole in a condensed form, I would like to make a brief recap of them here. At this point, I believe that the following premises will provide the basis for all future journeys for me.

The Relational Society Is Here

The first premise is that we are on the threshold of what I call the relational society. This conviction was the basis for my most recent book, *The Relational Revolution*. There is ample evidence that we are at the end of the Industrial Age and at the beginning of a new epoch—an intimate society—a time when the quality of life will be more important than goods manufactured or products consumed. The Relational Society, in Christian terms, might look something like the Messianic Age described in the Bible.

Until recently, our national mind-set has been toward expansion. We have thought in terms of unlimited growth of all kinds, of life without limits. Now, because we are living with the realities of the population explosion, the shortage of fossil fuels and raw materials, and the beginnings of serious ecological problems, we are beginning to see that we must live with limits. Bigger is not always better. In the past, our education has been aimed primarily at teaching us how to manipulate things, resources, and material objects. Perhaps our space and moon explorations are somehow the culmination of this prior age.

But in the time ahead inner space and inter-space will become just as important, if not more important, than outer space. Who we are and what is happening to us in our relationships with others is more exciting and potentially more rewarding than the control and manipulation of objects, however large or distant.

Recently, my wife and I flew from Fort Myers, Florida, to Minneapolis. Before we were even airborne, these words came over the loudspeaker system. "A very good morning to you all. How are you today? We hope you will have the most pleasant flight possible on this beautiful, warm, winter morning. Before we start our journey and serve you breakfast in the sky, would you look around at who is seated on your right and left, and possibly even in front or behind you? Get acquainted with these people. Find out their names and where they're going and enjoy the trip with them."

The whole plane began to buzz as passengers shook hands and talked to one another. Later on I looked up the stewardess responsible for the announcement and said, "What a great idea that was. Is that new company policy?"

"Are you kidding?" she said. "It's my idea. I just want flying to be more fun. You know, actually all airlines are pretty much the same. We fly the same equipment, we serve the same plastic meals, and we are subject to the same late schedules. The only difference is whether or not traveling is fun. I just try to make this the most enjoyable trip possible."

Obviously, this girl has some understanding of the idea of the relational society. In a time when air fares are regulated and equipment is standardized, just about the only variance is the relational quality of the trip. I am convinced, too, that this principle is just as true in merchandising. We go to stores where it is fun to shop, where the clerks are helpful and the atmosphere is pleasant.

It seems apparent, too, that all churches are not the same. Similar theology may be offered from the pulpits, but while in one church the hearers come alive, grow, laugh, cry, and minister to each other, in another there seems to be a conspiracy of unreality and irrelevance and a good deal of emotional constipation. The same gospel can bring different responses. After all, it is the quality of life that marks the authentic Christian. Jesus said, "I came that ye might have life and have it more abundantly" (John 10:10).

We Are Not Complete

My second premise is that we are all unfinished products. So it is with the whole man in Christ. Each of us is still an unfinished product, incomplete in this world. No one can be taken for granted. To me, this view of man is infinitely hopeful and the implications are unlimited and dynamic. If I believe that I "have it all" spiritually and I am still restless, unfulfilled and unhappy, then despair is natural and inevitable. But, if I know that my spiritual life, however radical and sudden its inception, is only a beginning of all that God has in store for me, I live with hope and expect growth.

In religious terms, goodness or righteousness is far more than the elimination of sin. The accurate meaning of the phrase "Be perfect" has to do with becoming the "perfect you," becoming all that we are meant to be. The word *salvation,* from the Greek *salus,* meaning wholeness or health, is more than being converted to Jesus Christ or attempting a sinless life or having an unwavering faith. The Bible says, "Work out your salvation with fear and trembling for it is God who is at work within you . . ." (Phil. 2:12, 13). From this perspective, no one is ever a finished product, and we can hold each other to unlimited growth.

We Are Responsible for Our Lives

While it may sound hard or unsympathetic, I have come to feel that seldom is anyone a victim in life. It seems to me that believing we have no choices is a major stumbling block to all creative psychology and can even hinder our understanding of the gospel. I have come to believe that one of the basic truths in the whole mystery of man is that we have the capacity to take responsibility for our own life. Each of us has chosen to a large degree to become what we are. Obviously, I am not referring to those who are economically depressed or politically oppressed but rather to those who feel victimized in the primary relationships of their lives—those parents, children, spouses, friends who feel unloved, abused, manipulated, minimized or slighted.

For example, my happiness should not be dependent upon the people around me who don't do what I want or who do what I do not want. Rather, my happiness and my completeness must come from within. At the same time I should not be miserable because someone I love doesn't seem to love me enough or has chosen to withhold love. To choose to love is to choose to be hurt. But the point is, I have the power to choose those who might love me and those who might hurt me. I do not have to be anyone's victim.

This seems consistent with the Christian gospel as well. You recall how Jesus dealt with the man beside the Pool of Bethesda (a forerunner of a modern sanitarium for the chronically ill) who had been sick for thirty-eight years. Jesus asked him, "Do you want to be healed?" The man's goodness, worthiness, or his ability to pay for services were never in question. The real issue was whether or not he would choose to live as a well person.

In answer to Jesus' question, "Do you want to be well?" the man immediately complained that he was a victim of his circumstances. He answered, in essence, "Sir, you've missed the point. You know this is a healing pool and that an angel from time to time disturbs the waters. The first person put in after that is healed. Well, for thirty-eight years, I've been counting on these four people to get me in first, and for thirty-eight years they have never got me into the water in time." Now we can only guess at what Jesus was communicating in his persistent question. But I think he must have been saying something like this: "Come off it! That's not the issue. I am offering you a chance to accept the benefits of health along with the obligations of health. Do you want to risk it?" Eventually, the man must have said yes, for Jesus healed him with the words, "Pick up your bed and walk."

It seems to me that we Christians especially need to reemphasize the power that each person has to choose his own lot in life. I believe there is truth in the old saying, "The hardness of God is kinder than the softness of man." I take that to mean that people in an impossible situation or relationship need something other than sympathy. They need someone to hold out hope, someone who will say, "Listen, friend, there is a great deal that you can do right now to change your life in a way that can affect your situation—physical, mental, or spiritual."

Naturally, there are some things in our lives that we are powerless to change. We cannot change our age, even though we may try to disguise it with cosmetics, face-lifts, wigs, and corsets. We cannot change our race or color, and we cannot change most of our physical characteristics, such as height or frame. But, in talking with hundreds of people over the years, I find that most of them are not miserable or sick or sleepless because of their age, height, or color. They are often miserable because of other things that are usually under their control. With God's help, most of the things that make us miserable can be changed.

Earlier references were made to the fact that Eric Berne in his book *Games People Play* speaks about the three roles that exist in all the games we play. There are "the victim," "the persecutor," and "the helper." Much of my unhappiness occurs when I feel that someone is making me a victim. But

I don't have to be a victim. I can change my role in that relationship and tell my parent, spouse, friend, enemy, or boss, "Enough of this!" At times I may be unhappy because I have chosen to be the persecutor, and, consequently, I suffer from guilt. Again, I can choose to stop playing this role. And finally, there are times when I may feel miserable because I have chosen to be the "helper" and my offers of help are rejected, taken for granted, or my helpfulness is either expected or exploited. Eric Berne reminds us that we can stop playing the role of helper and simply be a friend or a lover. I can choose to love rather than to play games.

We Can't Make It Alone

Next, I have come to believe that we cannot make it alone. We are all programed with two basic needs; the need for God and for a few other people.

As a Christian, I believe we are programed to belong to God. We have a God-shaped blank that can be filled by nothing, no one other than God. As a Christian, I make that statement on faith, but I believe it is psychologically sound as well.

First of all, our basic problem, as I see it, has to do with guilt. It is impossible to live in this life without accumulating guilt. Now, I am not talking about guilt feelings. Whether induced by self or others, these are signs of our neuroses. I'm referring here to real guilt; the knowledge deep inside of us that we have failed others by acts of omission and by acts of commission. We have betrayed; we have lied; we have manipulated; we have withheld; we have humiliated; we have judged. At the same time, I believe that forgiveness and redemption are possible only through God's love in the death and resurrection of Jesus Christ. He has dealt not with our guilt feelings, as destructive as they are, but with the fact that all of us stand guilty before him and one another. As Christians, our greatest witness to the world is our acknowledgment that by Christ's act of love and sacrifice, the redeemer of the universe says, "You are forgiven. You are loved. You are home free. I have paid the price. Go and sin no more."

We Christians have a message to share which is timeless and relevant and clinically sound. It is the message that people are loved by God and their guilt has been dealt with and forgiven. For this reason I believe that the search for wholeness must include coming to grips with the revelation of God in Christ. The finest psychological resources cannot help man with his basic need for forgiveness.

Another major point: I have observed from a clinical perspective that a belief in God helps us find our true purpose, our identity, and our direction. For example, even the secularists are discovering today the importance of hope. Hope, according to the futurologists, psychologists, and the human potential people, is one of the greatest life-giving resources we have. But it is interesting to reflect on the fact that hope is almost never based on something concrete. Hope is a dream, a dream which I believe comes ultimately from the mind and heart of God. To be a Christian is to be one who can actively tap that hope and begin to dream about one's own potential, the potential of others, and the potential for society. So, God is essential to any model for wholeness. God alone can deal with our guilt and God alone gives us adequate purpose, identity, direction, and a reason to hope.

We find this question in 1 John 4:20: "How can you love God whom you have not seen if you do not love your brother whom you have seen?" If God is our father, we automatically have a family and need that family as much as we need God. Jesus said to his disciples, "Whatever you bind on earth, shall be bound in heaven, and whatever you loose on earth shall be loosed in heaven" (Matt. 18:18, RSV). I take this to mean that we are to become that band of brothers and sisters who are responsible for the unloosing and liberating of one another.

I believe that belonging intimately to a few other people is essential to wholeness for a number of reasons, many of which we discussed in the last two chapters. The Bible, for example, urges us not only to confess our sins before God but to "confess [our] sins one to another that [we] may be healed," and to remember that "if we confess our sins he is faithful and just to forgive us our sins and to cleanse us from all unrighteousness." Apparently, forgiveness comes only from God, but the cleansing process takes place at the hands of one another.

In addition, I need to be accountable to people if I am sincere in wanting to see genuine change in my life. Some of us are overachievers and others of us are underachievers. But by being accountable to a continuing group of other persons, growth takes place. The Bible says that part of the good news is, therefore, that we are "no longer strangers and sojourners but members one of another."

The Creative, Therapeutic Power of the Nonprofessional

In recent years I have been overwhelmed by the evidence of the creative and therapeutic power of ordinary, untrained people acting as resource persons for others. Indeed, I see this as a hope-reality that points to a new direction in all the people-serving professions. We read in Matthew 10:5 that Jesus sent out the twelve, commissioning them to "preach as you go, saying the kingdom of heaven is at hand. Heal the sick, raise the dead, cleanse the lepers, cast out demons." I believe these words were not only to the apostles but to all who are believers.

We are now becoming aware of the power of the laity to serve Christ and his church in most areas of ministry. What I am hoping is that the church will see that our commission is not just to use the laity as leaven for the church structures, but the secular structures as well. The Church of The Saviour, where every member is ordained to serve God and man in the secular structure where he is employed, may well be a model for the future church.

A Positive Approach to Wholeness

In medicine we have recognized a new focus which defines health as being more than the absence of illness. It seems to me this is a needed new direction for all the people-helping fields. For most people life is enriched and increased not by just eliminating evil but by adding good. I am not suggesting we ignore pathology. Certainly there are times when people are medically or physically or spiritually ill and need help from experts who deal with disease or pathology. But, we cannot be merely anti-illness, we must be pro-health. In religious terms, it is not enough to be anti-sin, we must be pro-man, pro-God, and pro-wholeness. I have often wondered if this is the sense of Jesus' injunction to "resist not evil." Certainly Jesus recognized the existence of evil and took it seriously. His own physical life was ended by the forces of evil. But perhaps he meant that when we pour all our energies into fighting evil, evil itself grows because of the lack of a positive counterforce.

In the personal realm, if I have a serious problem, it grows out of all proportion when I become preoccupied with it. Fighting insomnia does not bring sleep. Hating shyness does not bring social poise. Trying not to think about food, does not help a dieter. I'm convinced that the philosophy of Alcoholics Anonymous is effective because it is not anti-liquor but pro-drunk. The old Scottish preacher, Thomas Chalmers, in his famous sermon, "The Expulsive Power of A New Affection," exhorted hearers to a relationship with Jesus as a way of overcoming life's crippling problems.

I suppose psychologically we owe a great deal to the idea of "peak experiences." Those with emotional problems are encouraged to isolate the peak experiences of life and are helped to enlarge their capability and capacity for such experiences. This is very different from the classic approach of clinical psychology which concentrates on helping patients eliminate the harmful and the destructive. Dr. Anthony D'Heuanno, who has been studying people who claim to have had such experiences, gives this account of his own initial peak experience.

"About two years ago I had an experience that became a turning point in my life. It began when I left Los Angeles one Sunday morning, hitchhiking my way up the Pacific Coast. I was leaving behind one of the most bizarre, intense, frightening, lonely, rich, challenging, tension-filled periods of my life. I had just completed a year's internship at a child guidance clinic as a prerequisite to obtaining by Ph.D. in clinical psychology.

"So, as I set out on the trip up the Coast, I had a feeling of completion and a feeling of impatience to be free from the stifling surroundings of the city. Somewhere past Santa Barbara, I started experiencing a peace and calmness perhaps unknown at any other time in my life. I was happy, joyful, delighted at being alive. I was excited and bursting with energy—physical, mental, and emotional. I felt almost totally free and unrestricted. My actions seemed more spontaneous and 'right' in the sense of being appropriate to the total situation. My thoughts were clearer, quieter and less conflicted than usual.

"I was much more aware . . . of an inner voice that told me what I wanted to do in any situation. I felt free to follow this voice . . . my senses seemed much sharper than normal; I felt that I was able to notice small details or subtleties . . . I had more appreciation of just being alive and of the entire universe, especially nature. . . .

"The ways in which I met and experienced others were very different from what I was used to. I was able to relate to the most varied and diverse people, many of whom had certain qualities or traits which I would have normally disliked or even have found abhorrent, with an almost continuous positive feeling."[1]

I have read many similar descriptions of "peak experiences" but nothing more definite and clear than this one. Health or wholeness or salvation must, among other things, be tied in with living in the way that D'Heuanno describes for longer stretches of time.

To me Martin Luther's admonition to "love God and sin boldly" is not license to sin but rather a plea to focus less on the negative and more on the positive side of life. If we believe we are forgiven by God (for the past, present, and future) we can then move boldly out into the arena of life to live it as it was meant to be lived. But no one has it made. The wisest, most mature, most educated or most astute among us is still not able to live most of his life as described by D'Heuanno in his first peak experience. This is not a permanently attainable goal. But we can learn how to live with an expectation of this kind of potential more of the time and believe this is what God wills for us.

But this requires a positive effort of the will. This seems our mandate throughout the Bible. In the Old Testament, Joshua advises the people of Israel, "*Choose* you this day whom you will serve. As for me and my house, we will serve the Lord." Jesus says in Luke 10:28, "*Do* this and you shall live." To live is to find the positive things we can do, the things that make for life, and choose to do them. We cannot avoid illness. We cannot avoid sin. As Christians we believe God will forgive us our sins as we confess them and repent from them and try to make restitution. Secure in this knowledge, we are free then to choose life and wholeness.

A *Sample Grid for Personal Growth*

It seems to me that we must have some sort of a spiritual, clinical, or theological grid through which we can see with clarity someone else's problems and potential and they ours. It is my intent eventually to put together a course which will offer a modular approach to personal growth and which will supply such a grid. Unlike the present curriculum approach with which we are all familiar and which puts everybody through the same learning experience, a modular approach would represent an individualized approach to each person's need and potential. As a result of my own study and research over the past years, I believe that any such modular approach should explore and encourage growth in at least eight separate areas, areas which we have already discussed in detail in former chapters. Any personal growth course should be tailored for those needing specific help in one or more of these areas.

1. *Choosing creative risk.* Wholeness includes the capacity for choosing creative risk. One of the universal symptoms of mental illness, apparently, is an inordinate need for safety. Certainly this need is symbolized and embodied in mental hospitals by doors which are locked, primarily "to keep the world out." Most of us need help in choosing and continuing to choose the creative kind of risk. I would say that at this very point the Christian life offers wholeness in that we are enjoined and encouraged to "lose our lives," to risk fame, fortune, and even life itself for the love of God and our brothers.

2. *Discovering authentic goals and values.* Many people are living unfulfilled lives because they have inherited goals and values to live by that are not authentically theirs. They have assumed the goals of their parents, of society, or of some other person or group. We can begin to help one another find those goals and values that are uniquely ours. As a Christian, there are certainly some clearcut goals and values that I accept as from God. But most of the choices that I face daily are not covered by the Ten Commandments or the Sermon on the Mount. I need to understand and cooperate with my own hierarchy of values.

3. *Finding an authentic lifestyle.* It may seem that there is little distinction between goals and values, and lifestyle, but I feel it is important to separate the two. Conceivably, someone with authentic goals and values could still be living a false, destructive, and even crippling lifestyle. There are many ways, for example, to pursue similar goals with different lifestyles. Two people who want to serve others through

the teaching profession, for example, can have identical vocational goals and widely varying lifestyles in terms of what they wear, what they drive, how they live, and where they live. It is essential to find a lifestyle that is congruent with what I am and with what I am attempting to be and do.

4. *Defining a healthy environment.* Healthy environment is another important part of wholeness—isolating what is a healthy environment for me and then setting in motion those things with which I attain that environment. By environment, I mean all of those things that surround me by my own choice; in addition to the obvious physical surroundings, there are vocational surroundings, aesthetic surroundings, spiritual surroundings (the church I join, the religious books I read, the conferences I attend). In the choice of geographic surroundings alone, one can move from the general, such as city or town, mountains or seashore, to the specific, such as apartment, house, or trailer. In which environment can I be most uniquely me, functioning in a maximum way?

5. *Learning relational skills.* This is one of the most basic and important parts of the grid of wholeness. By relational skills I mean understanding and practicing those attitudes and behaviors which make a relationship work. We are instructed as Christians to love and forgive our enemies and we can, by the power of God, learn to do that. But, more basically, how can I relate to my enemies in a way that demonstrates love and forgiveness without turning them off?

Even with our dearest friends or most intimate family members whom we love with our whole hearts, it is possible to act in ways that break the relationship and alienate the other person. Functioning with relational skill simply means learning behavior that is congruent with our feelings and convictions, whether in a family or on a committee.

In developing relational skills, I become sensitive to what it is I communicate or contribute in a relationship, whether it is an intimate one between husband and wife, parents and children, or a relationship with others on a job or committee.

6. *Understanding and enjoying your body.* We all have

presently some relationship with our body. We can be under its slightest whim and pampering it beyond reason. We can hate our body—its appearance, its uncertain functioning. We can be fearful and apprehensive about our body. Some of us consider the body unspiritual. We deny it, repress it, or beat it into submission. Actually, our body is part of us and one of the best friends that God has given us. Our body is to be cared for, to be enjoyed as a source of wisdom and learning. Through pain and illness, our body often suffers our unresolved psychic conflicts and acts in a way to protect and alert us. In a sense, it is suffering in our place, and that's friendship at its best. One can choose to make a friend of one's own body and be immeasurably enriched.

7. *Cultivating the intuitive dimension of the mind.* There are two sides to the brain; one is identified with the rational and the other with the intuitive. From all evidence, most people tend to rely entirely on just one of these two sides. Wholeness includes the full functioning of both sides of the brain. If we can react only rationally or only intuitively, life is diminished. God meant us to be both rational and intuitive creatures. In our Western culture it is perhaps the intuitive side that is more often the forgotten child. The average person living in this time and place in history has a special need to develop the intuitive and to learn to listen to the nonrational forces within as well as without. For the Christian, the intuitive can often be identified as the very voice of God within who will speak and direct in that still small voice.

8. *Developing emotional wholeness.* The human potential movement has done a good deal in the past decade to make resources available to people for exploring their true emotions. Even Christians are discovering that emotions themselves are neither good nor bad; they are amoral. But emotions denied or repressed become powerful forces that drive us to harmful and bizarre acts. As the mind and the body are God's good gifts to us, so our feelings are meant to work for us and not against us. A great many of us need help

first of all in recognizing our emotions and then in accepting those emotions. This does not mean living at the mercy of one's emotions, which is the stance of the classic neurotic, but rather to make emotions work for us as we make choices in the things that matter.

A Personal Process

Life is an incredible gift and a dynamic process which is never completed in this world and which even man's old enemy, death, cannot terminate. Salvation is simply God's costly intervention in our corporate and personal life to deliver us from destroying, ignoring, defacing, or abusing that gift. You and I are either in that process of salvation, with tremendous potential for growth and life, or we are resisting! We are not victims, we have the power to choose those things which make for health and growth. God will help us in this process and we can help one another as well. Wholeness, like salvation, is personal and individual. In all the areas we've mentioned, we can claim a personal and individual process of growth toward that wholeness using each other as resources in the process of becoming.

Socrates said that the unexamined life is not worth living. Earl Loomis in his book *The Self and Pilgrimage* says that "a failure to search for one's self is, in its crippling effects, little better than suicide. It is also a denial of neighbor and of God."

To understand the opportunities that may lie before us in these new times, we must wrestle with the ultimate questions that have confronted people throughout history: "Who am I?" "Where did I come from?" "What am I supposed to do and be?" "What does it mean to love another . . . myself . . . God?" These are theological questions. They transcend the social, the psychological, and the political, because life, ultimately, is theological.

We in the Western world must continue to work and fight for the economic, educational, and political freedom of all men everywhere. But we must be sure that we fight for more than that, lest we merely make man in our affluent and overprivileged image. It is our mandate and mission ever to continue the search for the meaning of the gift of life, always aware that ultimately that gift is a mystery. It has been said about war that it is too important to be left to the generals. So our quest for the meaning and the mystery of being human is every person's quest. I am my neighbor's partner and resource in the search and he is mine.

Notes

Chapter 1

1. Lecture, Kalamazoo College, October 13, 1970.
2. Thomas A. Harris, *I'm OK—You're OK* (New York: Harper & Row, 1967).
3. Frederick S. Perls, Big Sur Recordings, San Rafael, CA 94903, Tape No. 2910.
4. Lecture, University of Massachusetts School of Education, April 9, 1973.
5. Lecture, University of Florida School of Education, May 14, 1974.

Chapter 2

1. W. Fred Graham, "The Pastoral Ministry: 1. The People," *Christianity Today*, February 16, 1973, pp. 4–7.

2. Frederick S. Perls, *Gestalt Therapy Verbatim*, ed. John O. Stevens (New York: Bantam Books, 1971), p. 45.
3. Marina Chavchavadze, ed., *Man's Concern with Holiness* (London: Hodder and Stoughton, 1970), p. 103.

Chapter 3

1. Viktor Frankl, Big Sur Recordings, San Rafael, CA 94903, Tape No. 4251.
2. Interview in Cuernavaca, Mexico, July 1974.
3. L. D. Pankey Institute for Advanced Dental Education, Du-Pont Plaza Center, 300 Biscayne Boulevard Way, Miami, FL 33131.

Chapter 4

1. Paul Tournier, *The Strong and the Weak* (Philadelphia: Westminster, 1963).
2. Konrad Lorenz, interview in *Psychology Today*, November 1974, pp. 83–93.
3. Ibid.
4. Stanley Milgram, *Obedience to Authority: An Experimental View* (New York: Harper & Row, 1974).

Chapter 5

1. John Gardner, *Self-Renewal: The Individual and the Innovative Society* (New York: Harper & Row, 1971).
2. Quoted in Sam Keen, "The Golden Mean of Roberto Assagioli," *Psychology Today* 8:96, December 1974, pp. 96–100, 102 f.

Chapter 6

1. Paul Tournier, *The Naming of Persons* (New York: Harper & Row, 1975), pp. 88–89.
2. *Harper's*, February 1975, p. 12.

Chapter 7

1. Nancy Covert Smith, *Journey Out of Nowhere* (Waco, Tex.: Word Books, 1973).
2. Marina Chavchavadze, ed., *Man's Concern with Wholeness*, p. 113.
3. Geoffrey Moorhouse, *The Fearful Void* (New York: Lippincott, 1974).

4. Perls, *Gestalt Therapy Verbatim*, pp. 2–3.
5. Ibid.
6. *Commonweal*, November 29, 1974.
7. Elizabeth Kübler-Ross, *On Death and Dying* (New York: Macmillan, 1969).

Chapter 8
1. Jules Henry, *Pathways to Madness* (New York: Random House, 1972).
2. Viktor Frankl, "The Existential Vacuum: A Challenge to Modern Psychiatry" (Big Sur Recordings, San Rafael, Calif. 94903).
3. The entire speech entitled "A New Model for Humanizing Families and Schools" may be obtained by writing Effectiveness Training Associates, 110 South Euclid Avenue, Pasadena, Calif. 91101.
4. *Parade* magazine, May 12, 1974.
5. Ted W. Engstrom and Edward R. Dayton, Christian Leadership Letter, April, 1975, 919 W. Huntington Drive, Monrovia, Calif. 91016.

Chapter 9
1. *Book World, The Washington Post*, April 1, 1973, p. 1.
2. C. S. Lewis, *Mere Christianity* (New York: Macmillan, 1964).
3. C. S. Lewis, *The Great Divorce* (New York: Macmillan, 1946).
4. Paul Tournier, *The Meaning of Persons* (New York: Harper & Row, 1957).
5. Elton Trueblood, *Your Other Vocation* (New York: Harper & Row, 1952).
6. Perls, *Gestalt Therapy Verbatim*, p. 24.
7. *Time*, April 23, 1973.
8. Ibid.
9. *Book World, The Washington Post*, April 1, 1973, p. 2.

Chapter 10
1. Emile Cailliet, *Pascal* (Philadelphia: Westminster, 1945), p. 131.
2. William Glasser, "Education and the Needs of the Whole

Person," lecture at Baltimore Festival of Hope conference, May 1974.
3. Meyer Friedman and Ray H. Rosenman, *Type A Behavior and Your Heart* (New York: Fawcett World, 1975).
4. *Family Weekly*, April 27, 1975, p. 21.
5. From *Images: Women in Transition* (Nashville, Tenn.: The Upper Room). By permission of the author, Donna Swanson.
6. Richard Selzer, *Mortal Lessons: Notes on the Art of Surgery* (New York: Simon & Schuster, 1976).

Chapter 11

1. "Newsline," *Psychology Today*, August 1977, pp. 26–27.
2. Menninger Perspective, Fiftieth Anniversary Edition, vol. 5, no. 4 (1975), p. 9.
3. Ibid., p. 11.
4. William C. Menninger, *A Psychiatrist for a Troubled World* (New York: Viking Press, 1947), pp. 526–33.
5. Tom Huth, "Ten Boxes of Dead Mice Could Be Us," *Washington Post*, February 8, 1973, p. B-3.
6. From notes on a lecture heard in London in 1973.
7. Smith, *Journey Out of Nowhere*, p. 106.
8. Henry Mitchell, "Of Death and Living: Finding Succor in a Time of Dread," *Washington Post*, May 25, 1975, p. F-1.

Chapter 12

1. Dr. E. Fuller Torrey, "The Psychiatrist Has No Clothes," *Outlook, Washington Post*, October 13, 1974.
2. Ibid.
3. Berne, *What Do You Say after You Say Hello?*, p. 88.
4. William Glasser, *Reality Therapy* (New York: Harper & Row, 1965), pp. 42–45.
5. Gerald Goodman, *Companionship Therapy: Studies in Structured Intimacy* (San Francisco: Jossey-Bass, 1972), chap. 1.
6. Thomas Oden, *Game Free* (New York: Harper & Row, 1974), chap. 3.

Chapter 13

1. Bertram R. Forer, "The Fallacy of Personal Validation: A Classroom Demonstration of Gullibility," *Journal of Abnormal and Social Psychology* 44:118.

2. Paul E. Meehl, "Wanted—A Good Cookbook," *American Psychologist* 11:263.
3. Perls, *Gestalt Therapy Verbatim*, p. 38.

Chapter 14

1. "Personal Growth—Volume II," 1711-A Grove Street, P.O. Box 1254, Berkeley, Calif. 94701.

Index

Index